PROPRANOLOL AND SCHIZOPHRENIA

THE KROC FOUNDATION SERIES

Volumes in the Series published by Alan R. Liss, Inc.

Volume 10: Propranolol and Schizophrenia
Eugene Roberts and Peter Amacher, *Editors*

Volume 11: Sleep Apnea Syndromes
Christian Guilleminault and William C. Dement, *Editors*

Kroc Foundation Series
Volume 10

PROPRANOLOL AND SCHIZOPHRENIA

Proceedings of a Conference
Sponsored by The Kroc Foundation
Held December 1976
at its Headquarters in the
Santa Ynez Valley, California

Editors

Eugene Roberts, PhD
Director, Division of Neurosciences
City of Hope National Medical Center
Duarte, California

Peter Amacher, PhD
Director, Conference Program
The Kroc Foundation
Santa Ynez, California

ALAN R. LISS, INC. • NEW YORK • 1978

Address all inquiries to the publisher:

Alan R. Liss, Inc.
150 Fifth Avenue
New York, New York 10011

Printed in the United States of America.

Library of Congress Cataloging in Publication Data

Main Entry Under Title:

Propranolol and schizophrenia.

(Kroc Foundation; v. 10)
Includes index.
1. Propranolol – Congresses. 2. Schizophrenia – Chemotherapy – Congresses. I. Roberts, Eugene 1920– II. Amacher, Peter. III. Series: Kroc Foundation. Kroc Foundation Series; v. 10.
RC483.5.P74P76 616'8'982'061 78-1781
ISBN 0-8451-0300-8

Contents

1st Row L to R: Peter Amacher, Ilana Blum, Eugene Roberts, Saniha A. Zaki, Seymour S. Kety

2nd Row: Kenneth Savard, Neil J. Yorkston, Abraham Atsmon, Samuel Gershon, Ronald Okun, John H. Biel, Steven R. Hirsch

3rd Row: Daniel Van Kammen, Lars Edvinsson, Ferris N. Pitts, John H. Gruzelier, Gerald D. Aurbach

Participants and Contributors

Peter Amacher, PhD
The Kroc Foundation
Santa Ynez, CA 93460

Abraham Atsmon, MD
Department of Internal Medicine B
Beilinson Medical Center
Petah Tivka, Israel

Gerald D. Aurbach, MD
Metab. Diseases Branch
NIH, NIAMDD
Bethesda, MD 20014

John H. Biel, PhD†
Experimental Therapy
Abbott Laboratories
North Chicago, IL 60064

Ilana Blum, MD
Medical School and The Faculty of Continuing Medical Education
Tel-Aviv University
Tel-Aviv, Israel

Lars Edvinsson, MD
Department of Histology
University of Lund
Lund, Sweden

Samuel Gershon, MD
Department of Psychiatry
New York University Medical Center
New York, NY 10016

John H. Gruzelier, PhD
Department of Psychiatry
Charing Cross Hospital and Medical School
University of London
London W6 8RF
England

C.W.H. Havard, MD
Halliwick House
Friern Hospital
London N11 3BP
England

J.E. Hardebo, MD
Department of Histology
University of Lund
Lund, Sweden

Steven R. Hirsch, MD
Charing Cross Hospital Medical School
Department of Psychiatry
London W68RF, England

Doris Hollander, MD
Friern Hospital and Whittington Hospital
London N11 3BP
England

Seymour S. Kety, MD
Psychiatric Research Laboratories
Massachusetts General Hospital
Boston, MA 02114

†Deceased

Ronald Okun, MD
Department of Clinical
Pharmacology
Cedars – Sinai Medical Center
Los Angeles, CA 90048

Ch. Owman, MD
Department of Histology
University of Lund
Lund, Sweden

David R. Pitcher, MD
Halliwick House
Friern Hospital
London N11 3BP
England

Ferris N. Pitts, MD
Department of Psychiatry
University of Southern California
Los Angels, CA 90033

Eugene Roberts, PhD
Division of Neurosciences
City of Hope National Medical
Center
Duarte, CA 91010

Howard G.S. Sergeant, MD
Royal Free Hospital and
Friern Hospital
London N11 3BP
England

Daniel Van Kamman, MD
NIH, NIMH
Adult Psychiatry Branch
Bethesda, MD 20014

Neil J. Yorkston, MD
Halliwick House
Friern Hospital
London N11 3BP
England

Saniha A. Zaki, MD
Halliwick House
Friern Hospital
London N11 3BP
England

1. Introduction

Eugene Roberts and Peter Amacher

A small conference was held in December 1976 to assess the potentialities for the treatment of psychoses and schizophrenia with propranolol, a drug commonly employed in the treatment of cardiovascular conditions. If this use of propranolol appeared promising to those attending the conference, it was hoped that progress could be accelerated in making treatment with this drug generally available. This was a matter of great urgency because of physically undesirable and psychologically adverse side effects produced in some patients treated with available tranquilizing drugs and the psychiatric ineffectiveness of these agents in others. Recently, immunological disorders have been detected in some patients treated with the currently used drugs. The unpredictable appearance of apparently irreversible neurological damage in the form of the so-called tardive dyskinesias in many patients receiving tranquilizing drugs has raised the frightening specter of the accumulation of a population of individuals who are both psychotic and permanently neurologically disabled.

The conference was built around detailed clinical presentations by two Israeli internists, Abraham Atsmon and Ilana Blum of the Beilinson Medical Center in Tel-Aviv, whose brilliant discovery opened this area of investigation, and by the British group led by Neil J. Yorkston and including John H. Gruzelier and Saniha A. Zaki that has exten-

Propranolol and Schizophrenia, pages 1–3

sively tested, confirmed, refined, and amplified the original findings in work at Friern Hospital in London. A report of the British group's double blind study of propranolol therapy, completed after the conference, has also been included. Neither group has been lavishly supported by grants, and both had been faced by some personal, institutional, and operational difficulties often encountered by true therapeutic innovators everywhere.

A number of research psychiatrists interested in this particular subject and in drug therapy of mental illness in general were invited: Samuel Gershon (New York University Medical Center), Steven R. Hirsch (Charing Cross Hospital Medical School), Seymour Kety (Massachusetts General Hospital), Ferris N. Pitts (University of Southern California School of Medicine), and Daniel Van Kammen (National Institute of Mental Health). Clinical pharmacology was represented by Ronald Okun (Cedars-Sinai Medical Center), medicinal chemistry and pharmacology by the late John H. Biel (Abbott Laboratories), the field of beta-adrenergic receptors by Gerald D. Aurbach (National Institutes of Health) and Lars Edvinsson (University of Lund, Sweden), and neurochemistry by Eugene Roberts (City of Hope National Medical Center). Robert L. Kroc, Peter Amacher, and Kenneth Savard sat in for The Kroc Foundation.

Throughout the proceedings emphasis was placed on the detailed discussion of the clinical results and an assessment of the validity of the findings. This was particularly critical because, up to the time of the conference, all of the studies had been open ones and, therefore, were subject to all of the usual criticisms directed at such studies. The discussions of mechanisms of action of the drug in producing the observed effects were kept to a minimum and generally were reserved until the last afternoon of the meeting. It was felt that the urgency of applying the practical, empirical findings, if valid, to human psychotic disorders greatly outweighed the immediate necessity of elucidating the exact mechanisms of the antipsychotic action of propranolol. Two areas possibly relevant to the antipsychotic effects of propranolol were, however, discussed at the meeting. One was Gruzelier's work on the orienting reflex in schizophrenics which was done in connection with the British group's trial of propranolol. Secondly, evidence recently has been adduced for an abnormal distribution of cerebral activity in chronic schizophrenics as indicated by an abnormal distribution of cerebral blood flow. The influence of catecholamine and other transmitters on the vasomotor function of cranial blood vessels was therefore discussed.

As the discussion proceeded, it was apparent that the group as a whole considered the results of sufficient promise so that the work should be rapidly accelerated to determine definitively the clinical utility of the approach. The conference at The Kroc Foundation was followed by meetings held at the City of Hope National Medical Center and at the University of Southern California School of Medicine. Both meetings were attended by interested members of the medical and scientific communities, and there, too, the work was subjected to critical and extensive discussion.

The participants decided that this small book should be published detailing their findings. It is not intended as a definitive statement, but rather as a progress report making these promising and provocative findings available to the medical and scientific community for further development and exploitation, or criticism and rebuttal.

We hope that many patients suffering from currently intractable psychotic disorders may be benefitted by the material presented.

The skillful and devoted efforts of Dorothy J. Heller in assisting in the editing of the manuscript for publication are gratefully acknowledged.

2. The Discovery

Abraham Atsmon and Ilana Blum

THE FIRST CASE – EFFECT OF PROPRANOLOL IN PORPHYRIA

In August 1969 a 27-year-old woman was admitted to the surgical ward of the Beilinson Hospital in Petah Tikva because of acutely severe abdominal pains. That same evening she was transferred to the Department of Internal Medicine mainly because of the reddish color of her urine.

The patient's history was compatible with porphyria. She suffered from excruciating abdominal pains, tachycardia, slight hypertension, renal insufficiency, paralytic ileus, neurological symptoms, and marked mental changes which were hysteria-like with possible acute organic psychosis. Laboratory examinations verified acute porphyria and more detailed examinations disclosed the form known as variegate porphyria.

The patient's condition deteriorated rapidly and inexorably. In spite of huge doses of chlorpromazine and Demerol she continued to suffer from very severe pains. The mental disturbances and neurological symptoms worsened, her kidney function declined, and she became frankly uremic. Her blood pressure continued to rise, and her heart rate approached 180/min. After a few days it became obvious that, barring a spontaneous remission, the prognosis for this extremely severe attack was very grave.

Propranolol and Schizophrenia, pages 5–38

Perusing the literature on porphyria we came upon the notion that some of the symptoms of acute attacks of porphyria mimic hyperactivity of the adrenergic system. With that similarity in mind, therapy such as surgical sympathectomy (1) and administration of reserpine (2) had been carried out, with disappointing results. Nevertheless, the idea of the existence of a "toxic" factor which stimulates the adrenergic system was never completely abandoned in the older literature.*

The general condition of our patient was critical. Further increases in the heart rate and the blood pressure were bound to add an additional serious burden on her vital functions. It was deemed justified, therefore, to try to reduce both the heart rate and the hypertension with propranolol, a widely used beta-adrenergic blocking drug. These drugs were introduced into clinical practice in the early 1960's and during the latter half of that decade rapidly found wide application.

Propranolol is a competitive inhibitor of beta-adrenergic agonists. The presence of an agonist will shift the logarithmic dose-response curve of propranolol to the right, so that the dose of propranolol required to achieve a certain effect is directly related to the concentration of the agonist. At the time of our first study (1969) a daily dose of 160 mg/day was considered to cause maximal beta-adrenergic blockade. In view of the hypothetical toxic adrenergic agonist surmised by some to be present in porphyria, we though it possible that the dosage of the competitive antagonist propranolol might have to be much higher than the generally accepted maximum.

This raised the problem of determining the appropriate dosage of propranolol required, since preparing a dose-response curve in our patient was not feasible. It should be pointed out that the generally accepted pharmacological criteria of beta-adrenergic blockade are based upon inhibition of beta-

*Editors' Note: Recently, striking support has been adduced for the presence of a "toxic" circulating factor in chronic schizophrenics (Wagemaker H Jr, Cade R: The use of hemodialysis in chronic schizophrenia. Am J Psychiatry 134:684–685, 1977). From work with 11 patients it is concluded "At the present time, our dialyzed patients are in a better state of remission than patients who are being treated with neuroleptics."

adrenergic stimulation caused by administration of beta-adrenergic agonists. We decided to administer propranolol in increasing amounts and established as criteria of adequate dosage that amount which would reduce the pulse rate to a minimum of 60/min and/or the high blood pressure to normal values. No upper limit was put upon the dosage of propranolol.

Treatment with propranolol was started with 30 mg the first day, 60 mg the second day, and 100 mg the third day. As propranolol dosage was increased, some improvement was noted in all of the patient's symptoms. During the fourth and fifth days 100 mg of propranolol was administered every 6 hr for a total of 400 mg/day, which at that time was considered to be a tremendous quantity. With this treatment a drop in pulse rate and blood pressure was noted, and concomitantly very marked amelioration of all the symptoms occurred, so much so that we began to have doubts about the causal relation between the clinical improvement and the administration of propranolol. We had expected a reduction in pulse rate and blood pressure, but we had not expected a complete clearance of the mental symptoms, the disappearance of all the neurological signs and abdominal symptoms, and the marked improvement in renal function. We considered the possibility that the attack of porphyria had spontaneously remitted during the period of propranolol administration.

In order to ascertain whether this was the correct interpretation of the unexpected dramatic improvement, we stopped propranolol therapy. Another reason for this decision was to avoid releasing the patient from the hospital with instructions to ingest daily 400 mg of propranolol, which at the time was regarded as an unwarranted and dangerous dosage.

About 5 hr after the last dose of propranolol, the previous symptoms recurred and intensified rapidly. Twelve hours after the last dose the signs and symptoms were of similar severity to those noted before treatment.

Reinstitution of propranolol therapy, 100 mg every 5 hr, led to nearly complete disappearance of signs and symptoms within 10–12 hr. After the daily dose was raised to 600 mg the patient felt perfectly well and her renal function returned to normal. For several months any attempt to reduce the dose of propranolol resulted in a recurrence of symptoms. Later it was found that the dosage could be slowly tapered off. This patient's detailed case history and the extensive laboratory examinations have been published (3).

At present the patient is still under observation. At times she has an exacerbation of porphyria, both biochemically and clinically. She then takes about 100–300 mg/day of propranolol, adjusting the dosage herself according to her subjective needs. We have since shown that administration of propranolol to this patient reduced urinary excretion of prophyrins and their precursors (4).

The observations in this first case may be summarized as follows: All the clinical signs and symptoms of a severe attack of variegate porphyria were successfully suppressed by high doses of propranolol. The reappearance of the clinical manifestations of the disease upon cessation of treatment and their renewed suppression after reinstitution of propranolol therapy indicated a causal relationship between administration of propranolol and suppression of the clinical manifestations of the acute attack of variegate porphyria.

Propranolol is a beta-adrenergic blocking drug, but in high concentrations it also has membrane-active properties (at that time termed "quinidine-like effects"). Which of these properties had caused the salutary effects? By what mechanism had propranolol influenced the symptoms related to the central and peripheral nervous system, and was this influence specific for symptoms caused by porphyria? Delving into the literature pertaining to the biochemistry of the brain and of psychiatric disorders we found a possible connection between our observations and the catecholamine hypothesis of affective diseases (5). Another tenuous thread was the observation of increased urinary excretion of catecholamines during acute attacks of porphyria (6).

THE SECOND PATIENT

A short while later, we used propranolol treatment in a second patient, a 23-year-old woman who had given birth to her first child 1 week before hospitalization. This patient developed an acutely severe psychosis 36 hr before admission. She was a relative of the first patient, and the family was aware of the possibility of porphyria because we had examined several of the members of this family for latent porphyria and had found it in some of them. Therefore, the family asked us to examine her for the possibility of porphyria.

On examination she showed extreme agitation and restlessness and indicated no contact, whatsoever, with her surroundings. She had obvious visual, auditory, and tactile hallucinations. Her thought processes and content were severely disturbed and her affect was inadequate. Our consulting psychiatrist made a diagnosis of acute post-partum psychosis. We thought at first that she might have porphyria, but general physical and laboratory examinations were negative. A Watson-Schwartz test was reported by the laboratory as possibly positive for porphyria. This was later shown to be in error, but it was a fortunate error. Acute attacks of porphyria are known to occur with slightly increased frequency during and immediately after pregnancy. However, only infrequently is an attack manifested solely by an acute psychosis. Nevertheless, we persuaded the psychiatrist to let the patient stay with us for 24 hr, and he agreed, though with extreme reluctance.

Treatment with propranolol was begun, 130 mg every 4 hr for a total of approximately 800 mg/day. A very marked improvement in mental symptoms was noted during the first 16 hr and complete recovery had taken place by the end of the third day. Five days after admission she was discharged with strict orders to continue taking propranolol according to the same dosage schedule.

After 24 hr at home the patient and her family decided that there was no need to continue taking so many pills around the clock since she felt perfectly well. The patient stopped treatment, and 12 hr later psychotic symptoms recurred. The next morning she was readmitted with the same symptomatology as during her first admission. After reinstituting treatment with propranolol she recovered completely within 48 hr.

In this patient, as with the previous one, we were struck by the very marked temporal correlation between reduction of pulse rate and blood pressure and amelioration of mental disturbances; these changes occurred concomitantly on the same day. This pattern has been observed by us repeatedly and will be discussed subsequently.

The patient continued treatment (130 mg every 4 hr) for 3 months. During the following 3 months the dose of propranolol gradually was tapered off. For these 6 months after her admission she lived a perfectly normal active life. After this period propranolol therapy was stopped, and there was no recurrence of psychosis. Since then she has given birth to another child without any complications. Extensive laboratory examinations showed conclusively that this patient did not have, and never had, prophyria in any form.

In summary, mental symptoms of our first two patients had apparently been favorably influenced by treatment with propranolol in high doses. The first was a patient with an acute attack of variegate porphyria in whom severe mental symptoms were part of a multiple system disease. The second patient had an acute psychotic episode after delivery. In both patients cessation of therapy led to a resurgence of mental symptoms within 12–24 hr and reinstitution of propranolol completely alleviated the psychiatric symptoms.

These remarkable and unexpected results and the wealth of information in the literature about the possible role of catecholamines in psychosis induced us to attempt further treatment of psychiatric patients with beta-adrenergic receptor blocking agents in high doses.

In retrospect, it seems that the limitations of our knowledge of psychiatry and the classifications of mental diseases may have been helpful to us in the development of this project.

SELECTION OF PATIENTS FOR CLINICAL TRIALS WITH PROPRANOLOL

In the course of reading biochemical-psychiatric literature and on the basis of our experience with our first two patients, we formulated several theses on which we based our therapeutic trials. It appeared that treatment with propranolol, like giving insulin to a diabetic, constituted symptomatic treatment only and did not influence the cause of the disease. It was obvious that the doses of propranolol required to obtain therapeutic effects were much higher than those used in treating cardiovascular problems. We would be treating symptoms and not syndromes or specific psychiatric diseases.

The patients admitted subsequently for clinical trials were selected according to symptoms only, disregarding psychiatric diagnoses. Obviously, this method of selection often caused raised eyebrows among the psychiatrists with whom we worked. We selected patients with the following symptoms: excitation, manic affect, anxiety, manic behavior, hallucinations, and withdrawal with tension (markedly withdrawn but exhibiting great inner tension by increased muscle tone and by facial expressions). We also treated patients who displayed marked anxiety and signs of peripheral adrenergic hyperactivity. All were severely psychotic.

Patients studied by us in these therapeutic trials were treated in the Gehah Psychiatric Hospital, which mainly admits patients with acute or subacute mental diseases. This work was done in close cooperation with the psychiatrists of the Gehah Hospital, chiefly Dr. M. Steiner, currently in the Department of Psychiatry at the University of Michigan Hospital, and Dr. H. Wysenbeek, Head of the Gehah Hospital.

The patients were chosen according to the criteria outlined previously. Although not all of the patients had all of these symptoms, all were severely psychotic. Each was hospitalized in a closed ward. Admission to the hospital was necessitated by severe mental disturbances and was unrelated to our clinical trials. Informed consent for the study was obtained from the patients' nearest relatives. During a 2-year period we treated 44 patients. Table I summarizes some relevant data on these patients.

After we gained some experience with the first group of patients, we adopted the following procedure. Before being admitted to the trial, each patient underwent a thorough physical and neurological examination in order to exclude individuals suffering from organic diseases. Propranolol therapy was started after an initial drug-free observation

TABLE I. Details of Patients Treated With Propranolol

Diagnosis	Total	Sex M	Sex F	Age (years)	Heredity
Schizophrenia					
acute*	11	6	5	17–27	7
chronic†	15	9	6	19–34	4
Postpartum psychosis	8	0	8	20–30	3
Manic-depressive, psychosis, manic phase	4	2	2	22–45	–
Unipolar depression, agitated	1	0	1	63	–
Psychosis, organic brain damage	5	2	3	17–39	3
Total	44	19	25	17–63	17

*A patient was classified as "acute" if for a whole year prior to the present psychotic episode he or she was gainfully employed or fully functional and had social contacts beyond the home.

†A patient who did not meet the above criteria was classified as chronic.

period of 4–5 days. Elaborate laboratory tests and psychiatric scoring were performed. The scoring systems used were the following: BPRS, Brief Psychiatric Rating System; IMPS, Inpatient Multidimensional Psychiatric Scale (Lorr and Klett); SPS, Symptom Profile for Schizophrenia; PA, Problem Appraisal; SER, Side Effects Records (VA-NIMH).

The scoring was performed by two psychiatrists of the team and by a psychiatric nurse. The first 15 patients were started on propranolol doses of 600–800 mg for the first day. In subsequent patients, the drug was administered at an initial dose of 20 mg and then increased in the following manner. On the first day, the following doses were given at successive 3-hr intervals beginning at 8 a.m.: 20, 40, 80, and then 100 mg for each of the remaining time intervals. On the second day a total of 1000 mg was given at the same eight time intervals in equal doses. On subsequent days, the total dose was increased daily by 400 mg and administered on the same schedule.

Each patient's behavior, pulse rate, and blood pressure were monitored every 1 to 3 hr. When behavior became markedly more normal or when the pulse rate dropped to 58–64 and/or the blood pressure fell to about 90/60, the daily dose was kept constant. In patients in whom treatment was successful, changes in these three parameters generally occurred at approximately the same time. In those patients in whom mental symptoms did not improve, dosage was adjusted largely according to the pulse rate and/or blood pressure criteria. Once the patient had become "stabilized" i.e., pulse rate about 60/min, blood pressure about 90/60 mm Hg, and improved mental symptoms, we kept the dosage schedule constant. Generally, however, after a few days both pulse rate and blood pressure started to rise slowly and the patient's mental condition deteriorated. We called this phenomenon "escape." When this happened, we increased the dose of the drug until stabilization was achieved again, generally within 1–2 days. This process of "escape" with a requirement for higher doses of propranolol occurred several times. Therefore, the dose at which stabilization was achieved initially was nearly always markedly less than the final one at which the patient remained stabilized. From this point on the amount of drug did not have to be changed for many months.

Propranolol was withheld if pulse rate or blood pressure dropped below the stabilized value, or if either the systolic or diastolic blood pressure tended to rise. In most patients, treatment could be reinstituted after 6–8 hr. In some patients only the blood pressure rose, slowly or precipitously, while the pulse rate remained about 60. Thus, this is not a phenomenon of "escape" as discussed above but a totally different phenomenon. At about the time this occurred the patient displayed a host of other symptoms which will be described later. Under these circumstances we gave 20 mg of phenoxybenzamine orally. In a few patients 1 mg of phentolamine was given repeatedly intravenously, because of sudden and pronounced elevations in blood pressure. In two patients who refused to take medication, propranolol was injected intramuscularly in 5-mg doses until improvement occurred and oral administration could be continued.

When the pulse rate and the blood pressure were satisfactorily stabilized at about 60/min and 90/60 mm Hg, respectively, and the patient's mental condition was satisfactory, the frequency of propranolol administration was changed gradually from 3 to 6 hr without changing the total daily dose, so as to give maximal convenience in medication after discharge from the hospital. If no marked improvement was observed within 3 weeks, treatment was terminated.

The overall results of treatment with propranolol are shown in Table II. Two-thirds of the patients showed marked to moderate improvement as a result of treatment with propranolol. In many of the patients in whom the treatment was successful, improvement was already obvious within the first 24–48 hr. The symptoms improved in the following sequence: anxiety, psychomotor hyperactivity, disturbances in thought processes, hallucinations, and finally the disturbances in affect. These improvements began simultaneously with the stabilization of the heart rate and the blood pressure at about 60/min and 90/60 mm Hg, respectively, as schematized in Fig. 1.

In all patients in whom treatment was successful, the pulse rate dropped to about 60/min, the blood pressure to about 90/60 mm Hg; and at approximately the same time or within 1–2 days the mental symptoms improved. At no time did we observe an improvement in mental symptoms without the drop in pulse rate and blood pressure. We do not think that the improvement in mental symptoms was a result of the drop in pulse rate and blood pressure, since a number of patients who did not improve showed the same cardiovascular effects.

In some patients, side effects necessitated stopping treatment before adequate dosages, as judged by pulse rate and blood pressure, were attained. These patients did not improve. This correlation between improvement and cardiovascular effects seems to us to be significant in understanding the mechanism of action of propranolol. In our hands only that dosage of propranolol which caused these cardiovascular

TABLE II. Results of Treatment With Propranolol

Diagnosis	Total	Marked improvement	Some improvement	No improvement
Acute schizophrenia	11	7	2	2
Chronic schizophrenia	15	3	5	7
Postpartum psychosis	8	5	1	2
Manic-depressive psychosis, manic phase	5	3	2	–
Psychosis due to organic brain damage	5	–	2	3
Total	44	18	12	14

effects had therapeutic action in psychotic patients. It is obvious that this dosage is much higher than that normally required to achieve beta-adrenergic blockade.

The therapeutic dose of propranolol varied markedly from one individual to another, ranging from 600–5800 mg/day. Taking into account the variations in absorption rates from the gastrointestinal tract, which may differ by a factor of 20, these large individual variations are not very meaningful. To investigate this point further one would have to attempt to correlate blood levels of propranolol and its various metabolites, especially 4-OH-propranolol, with therapeutic efficacy.

Cessation of therapy led to recurrence of the psychotic symptoms within 6 to 24 hr. The symptoms usually, but not always, receded within 24 to 48 hr upon reinstitution of treatment.

No general depression of mental faculties was noted in patients who continued with high doses of propranolol. In particular, there was no impairment of intelligence, libido, or sexual functions. Motor retardation was not observed, nor were there Parkinsonian symptoms. Treatment with propranolol was least effective in those patients classified as chronic schizophrenics and in those patients with psychotic symptoms attributable to organic brain damage.

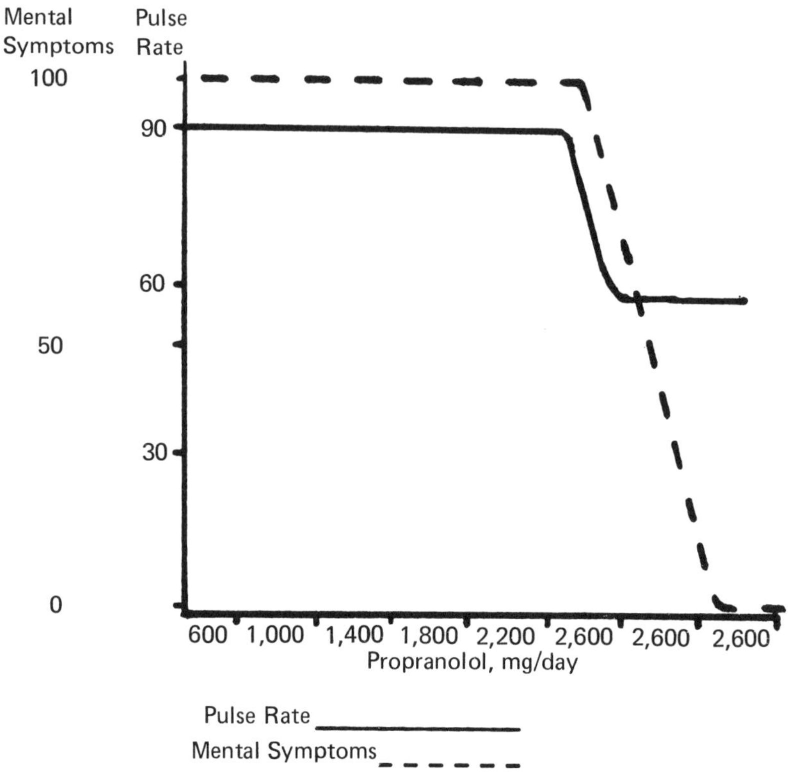

Fig. 1. The effect of increasing dosage of propranolol on pulse rate and mental symptoms. The drop in blood pressure occurred concomitantly with the drop in pulse rate.

SOME REPRESENTATIVE CASES

The complexity and variety of our experiences with propranolol can best be illustrated by anecdotal accounts of several individual cases.

Case 1

A 23-year-old woman was hospitalized suffering from hebephrenic schizophrenia. Before we saw her she had been treated unsuccessfully for an 18-month period with phenothiazines. Upon admission she suffered from disturbances of thought processes and content. Her affect was inadequate and labile. She had visual, auditory, olfactory, and tactile hallucinations and symptoms of depersonalization. Propranolol therapy was begun 4 days after cessation of phenothiazine treatment. The dosage was increased from 100 to 1600 mg/day within 5 days. We observed improvement on the second day after starting treatment, i.e., she realized that the voices she heard were not real but were symptomatic of her illness. A week after treatment was begun she was rid of the hallucinations but still showed a lack of adequate affect. The following week the dose of propranolol was gradually decreased to 800 mg/day, after which the patient was discharged. Since then she has never been rehospitalized, but an attempt to lower the dosage brought on a renewal of auditory hallucinations, which disappeared when the dose was returned to 800 mg/day. Eventually we succeeded in reducing the dosage, and currently 6 years after starting treatment with propranolol, she is maintained on 400 mg/day taken in four equal doses. The only psychopathology still remaining is a blunting of affect. According to the patient herself, reduction in dosage results in "bad thoughts."

Case 2

A 30-year-old man was admitted suffering from a manic episode. For 5 years he had manic-depressive psychosis, each manic phase lasting for at least 4 months and being followed within a few weeks by a depressive phase of equal duration. When we saw him he was in a manic period which had lasted 2 months, during which time he was unsuccessfully treated with phenothiazines. This was at a time when lithium still was not in general use in Israel.

Before commencing propranolol therapy, all medication was stopped for 2 weeks. Then, treatment with 800 mg/day of propranolol was begun, and significant improvement was observed after 24 hr. As usual with this form of therapy, insight preceded full recovery. He was discharged after 3 days and returned to work.

Against our explicit instructions he stopped taking the drug, since he considered himself to be fully recovered. Manic symptoms recurred within 24 hr and were relieved by reinstitution of treatment with propranolol. The same sequence of events was repeated twice. Because of the patient's unreliability treatment was stopped. The results obtained during propranolol therapy can be considered to have been most promising in this patient.

Case 3

A young woman underwent total thyroidectomy because of thyrotoxicosis at the age of 19. Since then she has remained euthyroid. She was seen by us at age 27 during the examination of a family with variegate porphyria and was found to have the disease in a latent form.

After the birth of her daughter 6 years previously, she was almost permanently hospitalized in mental institutions because of hebephrenic schizophrenia. She was treated with high doses of chlorpromazine, prochlorperazine, and other drugs, singly and in various combinations. Because of fairly severe extrapyramidal side effects, she also was given Dissipal and Artane. In spite of the drug therapy, she continued to have auditory and visual hallucinations and was functionally completely incapacitated.

She was started on propranolol, 800 mg/day, after 1 week during which no drugs were given. Two weeks after the beginning of treatment she was free of psychotic symptoms and resumed normal daily activities. During the following 2 years, the dose of propranolol was gradually tapered off to 320 mg/day. When she tried to reduce the dose still further, she experienced renewal of auditory and visual hallucinations, which disappeared after again raising the dosage. This cycle was repeated several times. The daily requirement fluctuated slowly between 150 and 350 mg/day. Too low a dose of the drug was followed within 24–36 hr by recurrence of psychotic symptoms, which receded after increasing the dose. Increasing the propranolol dosage was followed several times by hypertension and the so-called "hyper-alpha" syndrome, which will be discussed later.

During the 6 years she has been treated with propranolol, tests for porphyria have been carried out repeatedly, especially at times of reduction of dosage of propranolol with or without recurrence of psychotic symptoms. At no time was activation of porphyria symptoms observed.

During this period of treatment the patient has led a normal life as mother and wife. Her husband was killed during the Yom Kippur War. She coped very well with her loss and now has supported herself and her children for the last 3 years. She has not needed any psychiatric help or advice, although she has a residual blunting of affect. She now takes 240–320 mg of propranolol per day in four daily doses. Until now we have not been able to withdraw propranolol entirely without recurrence of symptoms.

Case 4

A 22-year-old woman had been under treatment for a period of 7 years suffering from schizo-affective schizophrenia with exacerbations and remissions. During the remissions she was unable to look after herself and during exacerbations she was hospitalized. She had received various forms of therapy, to no avail.

Because of an acute exacerbation she was admitted to the hospital at 8 p.m. Her pulse rate was 82/min and blood pressure was 120/80 mm Hg. She was extremely excited, had no contact whatsoever with her surroundings, and was obviously beset with threatening auditory, visual, and tactile hallucinations. She had to be restrained to prevent self-inflicted injury. At 9 p.m. we succeeded in giving her 100 mg of propranolol orally. At midnight, still restrained and showing slightly less agitation she received another dose of 100 mg. At 4 a.m. she was much quieter, no longer requiring restraint, and accepted further medication readily.

By 8 a.m. the acute exacerbation with all its symptomatology had receded and the patient wanted to go home. During the night her pulse rate had dropped to 60/min and her blood pressure to 90/60 mm Hg. During the following 3 days the patient received about 800 mg of propranolol daily and remained as well as before this acute exacerbation. On the fourth day of treatment she began to vomit after receiving medication, and the amount of propranolol retained became progressively smaller. We were unable to stop the vomiting, and within 3–4 days her condition deteriorated to what it had been on admission. We next administered propranolol intramuscularly, considering 5 mg by this route of administration to be equal to 100 mg given orally. The patient improved within 24 hr, remained well on the same regime for a few days, and then deteriorated once more. Intramuscular injections of propranolol caused massive indurations, leading to impaired absorption of propranolol. Again we had to stop treatment, the patient relapsed completely, and was then given conventional forms of therapy by the psychiatrists.

Case 5

A 38-year-old woman who had been a chronic schizophrenic with acute episodes for 17 years was admitted because of an acute exacerbation. After 10 days of treatment with propranolol she was released in relatively good condition, with instructions to continue taking the drug.

Two weeks later she was readmitted in a catatonic state. Her relatives informed us that, feeling well, she had stopped taking propranolol 2 days previously. Because of her catatonic state it was decided to give propranolol intravenously. Since we were concerned about the possibility of a hypertensive attack we were prepared with phentolamine, and two doctors and a nurse were present at all times. In addition, continuous electrocardiographic monitoring was instituted. Within 3–4 hr the patient was aroused from her catatonic stupor. Then, suddenly, her blood pressure, which during the infusion with propranolol had fallen to 90/60 mm Hg, started to rise rapidly while the pulse rate remained at 60/min. We stopped administration of propranolol and gave phentolamine by infusion. The blood pressure dropped, but within 30 min she became catatonic. Reinstitution of propranolol infusion led to exactly the same sequence of events, a cycle which was repeated four times. Finally, in the early evening, we stopped the treatment.

Repeated attempts to administer propranolol by stomach tube were unsuccessful. Subsequently the patient was treated conventionally by the psychiatrists and released from the hospital 6 months later.

SIDE EFFECTS OF PROPRANOLOL TREATMENT

We encountered only a few of the various side effects of propranolol (7, 8). In general, we had to deal with exaggerated pharmacological effects of the drug (9), namely bradycardia and hypotension. These phenomena subsided within 6–8 hr of withholding treatment. At no time did these effects present a significant problem. Other side effects encountered were due to allergy to the drug (skin) or to its effects on the gastrointestinal, neurologic or cardiovascular systems.

Skin

In one patient a slight skin eruption was observed during treatment with propranolol. When the drug was withdrawn the eruption disappeared but recurred upon reinstitution of treatment, after which the administration of propranolol was stopped. The eruption occurred at a relatively low dosage, 300 mg/day. No beneficial therapeutic effect of propranolol was obtained.

Gastrointestinal

The gastrointestinal side effects consisted mainly of diarrhea and vomiting. While diarrhea was never a serious problem, treatment had to be stopped in one patient because of persistent vomiting, and was resumed by administering propranolol intramuscularly. This form of therapy was also discontinued because of the formation of massive induration at the sites of the injections. The marked amelioration in psychiatric status subsided after stopping treatment and the patient became psychotic again within 24 hr.

Neurologic

Many patients reported tiredness and vivid dreams during the first 1–3 days. Some of them reported hypnagogic hallucinations. When this occurred while the patients had insight they were not overly disturbed or worried by this phenomenon. At no time did this necessitate discontinuation of treatment.

A more disturbing symptom was impaired coordination and ataxia. Some patients exhibited a "waddling gait;" some experienced difficulty in buttoning their clothes. In others slurred speech was noted. These phenomena disappeared by continuing treatment at slightly reduced dosages. In two patients the ataxia was more severe, and in four patients it preceded the appearance of toxic psychosis.

During toxic psychosis the patients had hallucinatory visions of small insects and animals and at the same time they suffered extreme anxiety and tension. Toxic psychosis was observed in 10 patients, two of whom also developed hypertension (Table III). Within 24 hr after treatment was stopped all symptoms of toxic psychosis disappeared. Generally, reinstitution of treatment at a slightly lower dose than that which had caused the toxic phenomena prevented their recurrence.

It is interesting to note that only two of the patients who developed toxic psychosis showed some improvement, whereas the others were treatment failures. This might indicate that those patients who experience toxic psychoses generally do not respond well to treatment with propranolol administered according to the dosage schedule outlined above.

Cardiovascular

One patient had premature ventricular contractions each time the pulse rate dropped to 60/min. When the drug was discontinued and the pulse rate rose to 80/min the premature ventricular contractions did not recur. In spite of the fact that the psychiatric status of the patient was greatly improved, propranolol treatment was stopped.

TABLE III. Patients Suffering From Toxic Psychosis

Diagnosis	Number of patients	Dosage of propranolol (mg/day)
Chronic schizophrenic reactions	8	300–1800
Acute schizophrenia	1	1000
Postpartum psychosis	1	1200

Another cardiac side effect occurred in a 49-year-old patient in whom mild congestive heart failure developed, which subsided after stopping treatment. In this patient, too, marked psychiatric amelioration was observed, but therapy with propranolol was stopped in order to avoid endangering the patient unnecessarily. Today we would have continued propranolol administration, adding digitalis and diuretics as required.

Both of these patients reverted to their previous severe psychotic condition within 12–24 hr after stopping treatment.

In eight patients a totally unexpected marked rise in blood pressure was observed during propranolol treatment. This rise in blood pressure was unrelated to the dose of propranolol (Table IV).

The hypertension was not related to escape from beta-adrenergic blockade since the pulse rate remained low, generally 58–62/min. In most of these patients the rise in blood pressure developed gradually, within 3–4 and up to 24 hr. In two patients an abrupt rise in blood pressure occurred within a few minutes, accompanied by other signs of hypertensive crisis.

In two patients the hypertension developed at the time full blockade was achieved, i.e., when the pulse first dropped

TABLE IV. Paradoxical Rise in Blood Pressure During Propranolol Treatment

Sex	Age	Daily dosage of propranolol at time of hypertension (mg)	Increases in blood pressure (mm Hg)
F	17*	5000	90/60–260/170
M	20	1200	90/70–160/90
M	23	2400	90/60–170/100
M	22*	1800	90/60–200/160
M	20	600	90/70–170/120
M	19	800	90/60–180/120
M	35	1000	90/60–160/90
F	32	600	90/60–180/110

*Patients developed hypertensive crises.

to about 60/min. In the other six, hypertension occurred on the day the dosage of propranolol was increased after a previous reduction which had caused a partial or complete release of the beta-adrenergic blockade.

During the hypertensive phase additional symptoms were noted in those patients in whom the hypertension developed gradually (Table V).

These patients were typically pale, cold, and clammy. They were withdrawn, but concomitantly exhibited very marked tension and sometimes uncontrolled outbursts of psychomotor unrest, often without apparent cause. These symptoms were noted either at the time of, a few hours preceding, or following the initial rise in blood pressure from the previous level of about 90/60 mm Hg.

The elevated blood pressure responded to treatment with alpha-adrenergic blocking drugs. In the patients with acute elevations of blood pressure and hypertensive crisis phentolamine was administered intravenously with immediate results as shown in Figs. 2 and 3. In those patients in whom hypertension developed gradually, phenoxybenzamine was administered in a dosage of 10–20 mg/day, reducing the blood pressure to the previous low levels. Along with a gradual reduction of the blood pressure the other symptoms abated as well. Treatment with propranolol was continued during administration of phenoxybenzamine. In a few patients in whom the mental symptoms appeared, phenoxybenzamine was administered and the expected hypertension did not occur.

We made another observation that may be of considerable importance. Administration of phenoxybenzamine to patients

TABLE V. Symptoms Concurring With Hypertension During Propranolol Treatment

Peripheral vasoconstriction
Tension
Withdrawal
Outbursts of rage and psychomotor activity with low threshold to external stimuli

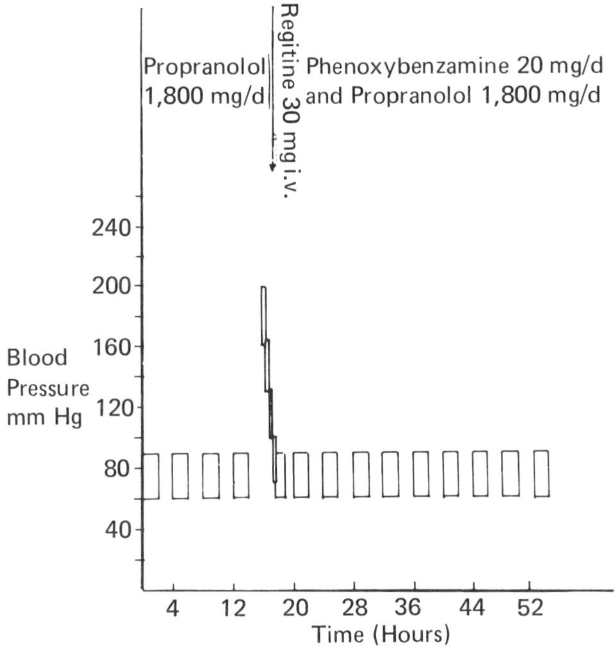

Fig. 2. Sudden rise in blood pressure and the effect of phentolamine (Regitine) in a psychotic patient treated with propranolol, 1800 mg/day.

receiving a constant dosage of propranolol always induced a recurrence or an exacerbation of psychotic symptoms.

In conclusion, taking into consideration the high doses of propranolol employed, relatively few side effects were observed. Among these, only two were of importance, hypertension and toxic psychosis. Hypertension was encountered only in the first group of 20 patients. When we learned to recognize the premonitory signs we were able to prevent its occurrence, either by slowly reducing the dosage of propranolol or by administering phenoxybenzamine. Thus, prevention of this potentially serious complication is possible by means of careful patient observation. Toxic psychosis was observed mainly in a group of chronic schizophrenic patients with low urinary catecholamine output. This correlation should be examined further in a larger group of patients. If this correlation is confirmed, toxic psychosis will probably be preventable

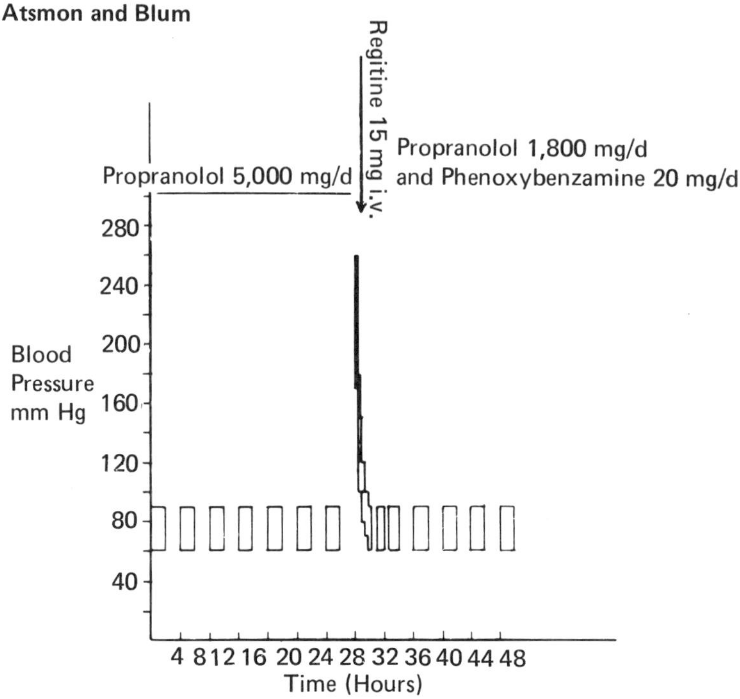

Fig. 3. Sudden rise in blood pressure and the effect of phentolamine (Regitine) in a psychotic patient treated with propranolol, 5000 mg/day.

by increasing daily dosages more slowly. Thus, it seems reasonable to assume that the two major side effects to the administration of propranolol by the dosage regime outlined above may likely be avoidable with more clinical experience and after additional laboratory investigations.

URINARY EXCRETION OF CATECHOLAMINES, CATECHOLAMINE METABOLITES, AND 5-HYDROXYINDOLEACETIC ACID

It was obvious that extensive laboratory investigations would be necessary to understand the mode of action of propranolol, to predict in which patients this treatment might be successful, and to prevent avoidable side effects. Because of limited laboratory resources we could only examine urinary excretion of catecholamines, some of the metabolites of catecholamines, and 5-hydroxyindoleacetic acid (5HIAA).*

In one such study a correlation (Table VI) was noted between the effect of propranolol treatment and of pretreatment urinary excretion of total catecholamines and 3-methoxy-4-hydroxyphenylglycol (MHPG) (10). Because of technical difficulties, we performed this study in only 12 patients. All the subjects were under 45 years of age and free of medical signs or symptoms. Seven suffered from acute and five from chronic schizophrenia. Twenty-four-hour urine collections were examined during the washout non-drug period, which lasted between 3 and 4 days. The urinary excretion of catecholamines, MHPG, vanillylmandelic acid (VMA), homovanillic acid (HVA), and 5 HIAA were made according to published procedures (11–13). Before treatment was started, each subject's psychiatric status was evaluated by means of an interview and scoring on the Symptom Profile for Schizophrenia (SPS).

Those five patients who were much improved by propranolol excreted high levels of catecholamines and MHPG in the urine prior to treatment and were acutely ill. Two out of the four patients who showed no improvement had an acute condition, but, nevertheless, had low urinary catecholamines. All patients who improved slightly under treatment or not at all had normal or low urinary catecholamines and, with the exception of one patient with no improvement, low levels of MHPG. If these preliminary findings are confirmed in a larger group of patients, a valuable method might be available for helping predict which patients might benefit from treatment with propranolol.

In another group of nine patients, three with acute and six with chronic schizophrenia, determinations were made of 24-hr urinary excretion of catecholamines, MHPG, VMA, HVA, and 5HIAA. In these patients the examinations were performed

*Editors' Note: There was general agreement among the participants that suitable measurements of the amine metabolites in the cerebrospinal fluid of patients before and after treatment would be desirable and potentially much more revealing of catecholamine metabolism in the central nervous system.

TABLE VI. Relation Between Clinical Outcome, Symptom Profile, and Pretreatment Urinary Excretion of Total Catecholamines and MHPG

Patients grouped according to clinical outcome	Number	Symptom profile for schizophrenia: $\overline{x}$ score		Urinary excretion of catecholamines (μg/24 hr)*		Urinary excretion of MHPG (mg/24 hr)	
		Pretreatment	Final	Average	Range	Average	Range
Much improved	5	13.2	2.4	259	143–422	1.34	0.92–2.51
Some improvement	3	14.3	7.0	111	79–160	0.535	0.46–0.61
No improvement	4	13.0	14.1	48	16–80	0.29	0.00–1.16

*The normal range of 24-hr urinary catecholamine excretion as determined in our laboratory is 80–110 μg, and of MHPG is 0.8–1.2 mg.

at the end of the 3- to 4-day washout period and again after 3 weeks of treatment. The above results were not disclosed to us until the end of the study. The patients were treated with propranolol and were rated by the various psychiatric rating methods mentioned previously. After the 3 weeks of treatment the psychiatric results were correlated with the pretreatment urinary excretion of catecholamine and indoleamine metabolites and the outcome of treatment with catecholamine and indoleamine excretion in the urine at the end of the treatment period.

All three patients who suffered from acute schizophrenia showed high pretreatment urinary excretion of MHPG, 5HIAA, VMA, and HVA, and all these parameters were reduced by treatment with propranolol. Three of the chronic patients who showed some improvement had normal pretreatment urinary excretion of the catecholamine and indoleamine metabolites. In those patients who benefitted greatly from the treatment, propranolol generally decreased the urinary excretion of MHPG, 5HIAA, VMA, and HVA, while this was not the case for the others.

In conclusion, our data show the following trends:

1. Patients with high urinary excretion of 5HIAA and catecholamines and their metabolites tended to respond better to propranolol than patients in whom the excretion was normal or low.

2. Patients with acute psychotic conditions generally excreted more catecholamines, catecholamine metabolites, and 5HIAA than patients with long-standing chronic schizophrenia.

3. Treatment with propranolol tended to reduce the excretion of the above substances in those patients showing marked improvement.

DISCUSSION

The overall results described were also observed by Volk et al. who administered oxprenolol (14), by Auriol et al. who used pindolol (15), and by Yorkston et al. who used propranolol (16, and this volume). These groups observed the same side effects we described, among others, an increase in blood pressure. Other investigators have not confirmed our observations (17–20). This possibly may be attributable to the small number of patients treated, use of a different dosage schedule, too low a dosage, or too short a trial period.

We deem several of our observations to be of special interest. There are several clinical situations in which hypertension has been observed during treatment with propranolol. Prichard and Ross (21) and Paton (22) reported hypertension in patients with pheochromocytoma. Nies and Shand, treating a patient with a combination of propranolol and alpha-methyl-DOPA, reported the same results (23). Hypertension has also been reported by McMurty (24) and Skinner and Misbin (25) during insulin-induced hypoglycemia. Because of the danger of hypertensive crisis, the latter authors regard the administration of propranolol in insulin-dependent diabetics to be contraindicated. Drayer et al. (26) observed increases in blood pressure caused by propranolol in a group of hypertensive patients with low plasma renin activity. Gabriel described the same effect when he administered sotalol, practolol, or acebutolol in rapidly increasing dosages to hypertensive patients (27). In experimental rather than clinical situations, hypertension in humans attributable to propranolol was observed in two situations: 1) during slow exogenous norepinephrine infusions (28), and 2) during insulin-induced hypoglycemia in nondiabetics (29).

The hypertensive action of propranolol seems to be the result of increased alpha-adrenergic activity caused by excess of catecholamines in the presence of beta-adrenergic blockade. This hypothesis is supported by the immediate drop in blood pressure noted during the administration of alpha-adrenergic blocking drugs. In some of these situations the increased release of catecholamines has a ready explanation, such as in states of hypoglycemia. In other circumstances, administration of high doses of propranolol could possibly induce release of catecholamines. In animal models propranolol also induces increases in blood pressure by releasing catecholamines from the adrenal medulla. This was observed in rats (30–32) and in dogs (33). The latter (33) also showed that central beta-adrenergic blockade with small doses of propranolol prior to administration of propranolol in high dosage prevented the release of catecholamines by the adrenals and prevented subsequent increase in blood pressure.

It seems possible, therefore, that the incidence of hypertensive episodes in propranolol-treated psychotic patients might be reduced by increasing the dosage slowly, instead of rapidly. If this is confirmed, one might surmise that by slowly increasing the dosage of propranolol those properties of the drug which inhibit synthesis and/or release of catecholamines (34–36) predominate over its unmasking of alpha-adrenergic receptors or the release of catecholamines by the adrenals and probably by other sympathetic nerves. However, a note of caution seems to be indicated. In all the above cited instances of patients with increased blood pressure during treatment with beta-adrenergic blocking agents, the doses of the drug were quite small as compared to those used in our studies. A stressful situation was apparently sufficient to produce the hypertension; in some patients increases in blood pressure seemed to occur "spontaneously," mainly in the low renin hypertensive patients (26). It is conceivable, therefore, that during treatment with propranolol, especially at high dosage levels, various kinds of stimuli may induce elevations in blood pressure. Indeed, we have observed hypertension in two psychotic patients treated by us with the slowly increasing dosage regime described by Dr. Yorkston in this volume.

The rapid mode of administration has the advantage of achieving therapeutic goals within a matter of days, but in the hands of an inexperienced physician many side effects may be expected. After we had gained the necessary experience, no serious side effects occurred. Thus, we feel certain that most of the side effects, and certainly the severe ones, are avoidable.

The slow method of administration requires considerable experience also, and therapeutic results are achieved at a slower rate. Using the slow method 2 of our first 10 patients developed hypertensive encephalopathy.

It seems to us that the choice of the fast or slow rate of drug administration must be determined for each individual patient. At present, we feel that chronic schizophrenics probably will respond better by slowly raising the dosage, but that in acute attacks the dosage rise can be faster. Laboratory examinations (blood levels and urinary excretion of catecholamines) and pharmacological tests (such as reaction to a test dose of intravenous propranolol or cardiovascular reactions to beta-agonists) may aid in the individualizing dosage regimes. Presently, we are convinced that the problem of dosage is a critical one and that many future investigations will have to be carried out before appropriate dosage regimes can be determined.

It is possible that, with improved pharmacological evaluations, psychotic patients who respond to propranolol treatment may be divided into three groups: 1) patients who will respond only to the "slow" method of treatment – mostly chronic schizophrenics; 2) patients who will respond favorably to the "rapid" method of treatment, but probably additionally may require alpha-adrenergic blocking drugs – mainly acute schizophrenics; and 3) patients who will respond to the "rapid" treatment with propranolol only – manic patients and acutely psychotic patients, such as women with postpartum psychoses.

Two observations were noted during propranolol therapy that seemed important. One was the close parallelism between reduction in pulse rate and blood pressure and the reduction in psychotic symptoms. The second was the complex of symptoms occurring simultaneously with the hypertension that sometimes arose during the propranolol treatment.

Generally, the psychotic symptoms in a particular individual receded at that dose of propranolol which lowered the pulse rate to about 60/min and the blood pressure to about 90/60 mm Hg. When, during treatment, the blood pressure and the pulse rate rose from the above values, an increase or a recurrence of psychotic symptoms usually was observed. We called this phenomenon "escape from blockade." This was our signal to increase the dose of propranolol until full beta-adrenergic blockade was attained again. This does not imply that the decrease in pulse rate and blood pressure caused the improvement in mental symptoms. A number of patients showed decreases in pulse rate and blood pressure without improvement in their psychotic symptoms. However, it does indicate that with our dosage schedule, propranolol affects psychotic symptomatology only when its pharmacological effect is sufficiently strong to reduce pulse rate and blood pressure considerably.

The cardiovascular effects of propranolol outlined above are thought to be caused by its membrane-stabilizing activity, and it might be conjectured that the beneficial action of propranolol on psychotic symptomatology also may be attributable to such effects. However, the above observation also can be interpreted differently. The very facts that huge doses of propranolol may be given to psychotic patients with impunity and that the pulse rate and blood pressure are reduced only when very high dosages are administered indicate that the cardiovascular system (and probably other systems as well) is reset at a different level than the normal one. This could be due to the presence of high concentrations of normal or abnormal beta-agonists or of stimulators of non-beta-adrenergic adenyl cyclases. In this event there would be a requirement for high dosages of propranolol either for competitive inhibition of the beta-agonists or for inhibition of non-beta-adenyl cyclase. The high dosages of propranolol required may indicate that some forms of psychoses are generalized diseases, the symptomatology of which is expressed clinically mainly by mental symptoms.

In some patients a rise in blood pressure occurred while the pulse rate remained low, 58–62/min. Concomitantly, the patients became pale, their skins were clammy, and marked changes in behavior were seen. The following were observed: 1) rise in blood pressure, 2) peripheral vasoconstriction, 3) tension, 4) withdrawal, 5) paranoid ideation, and 6) outbursts of rage and psychomotor activity with low threshold to external stimuli.

This symptom complex (which we dubbed "hyper-alpha syndrome") receded when alpha-adrenergic blocking drugs were administered. Since both the peripheral and the mental symptoms respond to alpha-adrenergic blockade, we feel justified in assuming that they are caused by a combined central and peripheral hyperactivity of alpha-adrenergic receptors unopposed by beta-adrenergic activity, which has been blocked by propranolol (37).

The "hyper-alpha syndrome" occurred only under two, well-defined circumstances: 1) at the time a patient, in whom propranolol dosage was raised rapidly, reached what we called full beta-blockade; 2) more commonly, when the dosage of propranolol was increased after a previous reduction in dosage and consequent "escape from beta-blockage" occurred. The moment the pulse rate dropped after having reincreased the dose of propranolol the "hyper-alpha syndrome" would appear.

The psychotic symptomatology which responded to propranolol consisted of anxiety, excitement, disturbances in thought processes, disturbances in affect, and hallucinations. This symptom complex was called the "hyper-beta syndrome." It is worthwhile stressing that the administration of phenoxybenzamine to patients on a constant dosage of propranolol at a time when they were symptomless led to recurrence of the "hyper-beta syndrome."

Thus we observed two syndromes: the original psychoses, improved by propranolol and worsened by phenoxybenzamine, and a syndrome which in some of our patients appeared during treatment with propranolol and was improved by phenoxybenzamine or phentolamine. This led us to postulate that normally a balance exists between the two systems which, when it swings to one extreme or the other, gives rise to the two different symptom complexes:

Hyper-alpha	*Hyper-beta*
Tension	Anxiety
Withdrawal	Excitement
Outbursts of rage and psychomotor activity with low threshold to external stimuli	Disturbances in thought processes
	Disturbances in affect
	Hallucinations

Accordingly, one may classify our patients into two groups. In the first group, hypertension occurred upon achieving full blockade. These patients were classified as having had initially *both* hyper-alpha and hyper-beta syndromes, with the latter completely masking the hyper-alpha syndrome. The hyper-alpha syndrome was unmasked when full blockade of the hyper-beta syndrome was reached.

The second group of patients initially showed only the hyper-beta syndrome. When full beta blockade was established with propranolol, release of catecholamines was blocked (the guanethidine-like action of propranolol), while synthesis still continued. This led to accumulation of catecholamines presynaptically. Upon "escape" from blockade, the organism was flooded with catecholamines and became symptomatic, i.e. hypertension, etc., and again asymptomatic upon reinstitution of full blockade achieved by raising the dose of propranolol.

Most patients never showed the "escape" phenomenon or the hyper-alpha syndrome. At least some of them may constitute a third group.

These hypotheses may be verified or refuted with appropriate laboratory procedures and/or pharmacological tests. Their testing has both obvious theoretical and practical therapeutic implications.

According to the above classification, both the alpha- and beta-adrenergic receptor systems may control different aspects of affect, but only the beta system appears to be correlated with thought processes and the interpretation and coordination of sensory perceptions. Psychosis would occur when the total adrenergic activity is either too high or too low, or when the balance is disturbed, one of the two systems being relatively either too high or too low. When the activity of one or both systems is too low, various syndromes characterized by tiredness, weakness, low psychomotor activity, apathy, or irritability could occur. Such syndromes do actually exist, but we do not know of any attempt to classify them in relation to the alpha- and beta-adrenergic systems. In one such syndrome, monoamine oxidase inhibitors have a beneficial influence. It seems to us that this may be a fruitful field for clinical and laboratory investigations with promising therapeutic potentialities. Similarly, a hyper-alpha syndrome, without hypertension, could probably be delineated and treated with alpha-receptor blocking drugs.

A relatively excessive stimulation of the beta system in certain brain areas might explain why the disturbances in thought processes and the hallucinations differ from patient to patient. Since the contents of thoughts and hallucinations would be determined by the areas in which the specific beta system stimulation is excessive, both "depressive" and "elated" (or "manic") thoughts may be due to a similar basic biochemical abnormality. Various forms of depression, especially "agitated depression," might, therefore, belong to the group of diseases resulting from hyperactivity in a certain area in the brain and might respond to large doses of propranolol.

The mechanism of the antipsychotic action of propranolol is still entirely unknown. Minimally, the following mechanisms may be involved: blockade of beta-adrenergic receptors, nonspecific inhibition of adenyl cyclase, nonspecific membrane effects, and inhibition of synthesis and/or release of catecholamines.

REFERENCES

1. Watson CJ: "Cecil-Loeb Textbook of Medicine," 11th ed. Philadelphia: Saunders, 1963.
2. Watson CJ: "Advances in Internal Medicine." New York: Yearbook Medical Publishers, 1954, vol 6.
3. Atsmon A, Blum I, Fischl J: Treatment of an acute attack of porphyria variegata with propranolol. S Afr Med J 46:311, 1972.
4. Blum I, Atsmon A: Reduction of porphyrin excretion in porphyria variegata by propranolol. A case report. S Afr Med J 50:898, 1976.
5. Schildkraut JJ: The catecholamine hypothesis of affective disorders: A review of supporting evidence. Am J Psychiatry 122: 509, 1965.

6. Schley G, Bock KD, Hocevar V, Merguet P, Rausch-Stroomann J-G, Schroeder E, Schumann HJ: Hochdruck und tachykardie bei der akuten intermittierenden porphyrie. Klin Wochenschr 48:36, 1970.
7. Stephen SA: Unwanted effects of propranolol. Am J Cardiol 18:463, 1966.
8. Morrelli HF: Propranolol. Ann Intern Med 78:913, 1973.
9. Nickerson M, Collier B: Drugs inhibiting adrenergic nerves and structures innervated by them. In "The Pharmacological Basis of Therapeutics," Goodman LS, Gilman A (eds): 5th ed. New York: Macmillan, 1975, pp 533–564.
10. Atsmon A, Blum I, Steiner M, Latz A, Wijsenbeek H: Further studies with propranolol in psychotic patients. Relation to initial psychiatric state, urinary catecholamines and 3-methoxy-4-hydroxy-phenylglycol excretion. Psychopharmacologia 27:249, 1972.
11. Euler US von, Floding I: Diagnosis of pheochromocytoma by fluorimetric estimation of adrenaline and noradrenaline in urine. Scand J Clin Lab Invest 8:288, 1956.
12. Wolf RL, Mendlowitz M, Roboz J, Gitlow S: Simultaneous urinary assays for the combined metanephrine and 3-methoxy-4-hydroxyphenylglycol in patients with pheochromocytoma and primary hypertension. N Engl J Med 273:1459, 1965.
13. Eichhorn F, Rutenberg A: A simple low-voltage paper electrophoretic method for the determination of urinary vanillylmandelic acid (VMA). Clin Chem 9:615, 1963.
14. Volk W, Bier W, Braun JP, Gruter W, Spiegelberg U: Behandlung von erregten psychosen mit einem beta-receptoren-blocker (Oxprenolol) in hoher dosierung. Nervenarzt 43:491, 1972.
15. Auriol B, Palandjian N, Bord M, Vals A: Les beta-bloquants en psychiatrie. La Nouvelle Presse Medicale 1:1439, 1972.
16. Yorkston NJ, Zaki SA, Malix MKU, Morrison RC, Havard CWH: Propranolol in the control of schizophrenic symptoms. Br Med J 4:633, 1974.
17. Hecht Orzack M, Branconnier R, Gardos G: CNS effects of propranolol in man. Psychopharmacologia 29:299, 1974.
18. Rackensperger W, Gaupp R, Mattke DJ, Schwarz D, Stutte KH: Treatment of acute schizophrenic psychosis with beta-adrenergic blocking agents. Arch Psychiat Nervenkr 219:29, 1974.
19. Stam FC: Enkele ervaringen met propranolol-behandeling van schizofrenen. Nederl Tijdsch Psychiat 13:424, 1971.
20. Gardos G, Cole JO, Volicer L, Hecht Orzack M, Cole Oliff A: A dose-response study of propranolol in chronic schizophrenics. Curr Ther Res 15:314, 1973.

21. Prichard BNC, Ross EJ: Use of propranolol in conjunction with alpha-receptor-blocking agents in pheochromocytoma. Am J Cardiol 18:394, 1966.
22. Paton DM: Beta-receptor blockade in the diagnosis of pheochromocytoma. Lancet 2:1125, 1964.
23. Nies AS, Shand DG: Hypertensive response to propranolol in a patient treated with methyldopa – a proposed mechanism. Clin Pharmacol Ther 14:823, 1973.
24. McMurtry RJ: Propranolol, hypoglycemia and hypertensive crisis. Ann Intern Med 80:669, 1974.
25. Skinner DJ, Misbin RI: Uses of propranolol. N Engl J Med 293: 1205, 1975.
26. Drayer JIM, Keim HJ, Weber MA, Case DB, Laragh JH: Unexpected pressor responses to propranolol in essential hypertension, an interaction between renin, aldosterone and sympathetic activity. Am J Med 60:897, 1976.
27. Gabriel R: Paradoxical rise in blood pressure during propranolol treatment. Br Med J 1:219, 1976.
28. Glover WE, Hutchison K: The effect of a beta-receptor antagonist (propranolol) on the cardiovascular response to intravenous infusions of noradrenaline in man. J Physiol 177:59P, 1965.
29. Lloyd-Mostyn RH, Oram S: Modification by propranolol of cardiovascular effects of induced hypoglycemia. Lancet 1:1213, 1975.
30. Regoli D: Pressor action of beta blocking agents in rats. Can J Physiol Pharmacol 48:481, 1970.
31. Yamamoto J, Sekiya A: On the pressor action of propranolol in the rat. Arch Int Pharmacodyn Ther 179:372, 1969.
32. Dasgupta NK: On the mechanism of the pressor response due to propranolol. Br J Pharmacol 34:200P, 1968.
33. Srivastava RK, Kulshrestha VK, Singh N, Bhargava KP: Central cardiovascular effects of intracerebroventricular propranolol. Eur J Pharmacol 21:222, 1973.
34. Adler-Graschinsky E, Langer SZ: Possible role of a beta-adrenoceptor in the regulation of noradrenaline release by nerve stimulation through a positive feedback mechanism. Br J Pharmacol 53:43, 1975.
35. Day MD, Owen DAA, Warren PR: An adrenergic neuron blocking action of propranolol in isolated tissues. J Pharm Pharmacol 20: 130S, 1968.
36. Hanbauer I, Kopin IJ, Guidotti A, Costa E: Induction of tyrosine hydroxylase elicited by beta-adrenergic receptor agonists in normal and decentralized sympathetic ganglia; role of cyclic 3′,5′-adenosine monophosphate. J Pharmacol Exp Ther 193:95, 1975.
37. Blum I, Atsmon A: The possible role of beta-adrenergic and alpha-adrenergic sensitive systems in the brain in the mechanism of psychosis. Med Hypoth 2:104, 1976.

3. The Second Stage—Confirmation and Refinement

3A. Propranolol in the Treatment of Schizophrenia: An Uncontrolled Study With 55 Adults

Neil J. Yorkston, Saniha A. Zaki, and C. W. H. Havard

INTRODUCTION

When we attempted to replicate in schizophrenic patients a method of using propranolol for psychosis in which the dose was raised steeply (1), our first three attempts were stopped by severe, acute toxic effects (2, 3). These occurred when we followed the regimen of giving propranolol in multiple doses (four to ten times per 24 hours), and of rapidly increasing the daily total by 400–800 mg/day (1, 4, 5). As a safer system was developed, toxic effects steadily decreased (6, 7). The measures responsible for reducing the toxic effects were: i) propranolol was usually given twice daily, ii) the daily total dose was raised by 40–80 mg/day, iii) propranolol was combined with a major tranquillizer rather than raising the dose too high, and iv) the staff became experienced in observing the early signs of toxicity and of improvement by which the dose was adjusted. No chronic toxic effects were seen (6, 7).

This paper describes the dosage and short-term results in our first 55 patients with florid schizophrenic symptoms treated with propranolol alone or propranolol combined with a major tranquillizer.

Propranolol and Schizophrenia, pages 39–67

METHODS

Patients

The 55 patients, 32 men and 23 women, were diagnosed by two psychiatrists as having schizophrenia with florid symptoms. Their ages ranged from 18 to 76 years; the median was 33 years (Table I). Thirteen had a paranoid illness in the sense of having a chronic, systematized delusional state. The 42 non-paranoid patients comprised one with a puerperal illness, five with schizoaffective psychosis, and 36 with hebephrenic schizophrenia.

Only patients who could safely be given propranolol were accepted into the study. For example, those with bronchial asthma or diabetes mellitus were excluded, and all patients in the study were given a test dose of 20 mg of propranolol to exclude an idiosyncratic reaction.

To be included in the study each patient had to score at least "moderate" (8) on two or more of the ten "schizophrenia" scales of a modified (2) Brief Psychiatric Rating Scale (BPRS) (9). At least one of these had to be one of the three "thought disorder" scales – conceptual disorganization, hallucinatory behavior, or unusual thought content. The seven "other schizophrenia" scales were blunted affect, emotional withdrawal, suspiciousness, grandiosity, mannerisms or posturing, hostility, and motor retardation. [Elsewhere this group has been called "non-thought disorder schizophrenia" scales (10, 11).] The scores from the "thought disorder" scales and the "other schizophrenia" scores were added to yield a "total schizophrenia" score.

Apart from the ten "schizophrenia" scales already mentioned, there were also nine "remaining" [or "non-schizophrenia" (10, 11)] scales: somatic concern, anxiety, guilt feelings, tension, depressed mood, uncooperativeness, excitement, disorientation, and pressure of speech. The last three items were added to the original BPRS. A further modification was to score the items from 0 to 6 instead of 1 to 7. A symptom that disappeared thus scored zero on the modified BPRS. Since "moderate" scored 3, the minimum "total schizophrenia" score was 6 (2).

Scores within each group of scales were added to give totals for the "thought disorder" scales, "other schizophrenia" scales, and "remaining" scales. The histograms (Figs. 1–6) show these totals for each individual before starting propranolol and at the last available rating when this report was compiled. The figures also identify each individual by case number, and show the duration of the total illness and of the current episode. The criteria for defining the onset and duration of illness were altered to those of the Schizophrenia Research Project (11). The illness was thus dated from the first clearly psychotic symptoms, and any "recovery" required at least one year "apparently symptom-free and functioning reasonably well in society" (11). [These stricter definitions account for some of the rearrangements of results between previous reports (2, 3, 6) and this. Further, the number of remissions has risen.] This information is in Table I which also shows each patient's sex, age of onset, age of starting propranolol, previous treatment, and, for the patients whose symptoms remitted, the dose of propranolol and other drugs at remission.

Questions about the "first rank" symptoms of schizophrenia (12) were asked in a structured interview. Because they were leading questions, if there was any doubt the symptom was rated as not present. Ten items were considered: audible thoughts, somatic passivity, thought insertion, thought withdrawal, thought broadcast, passivity of feelings or impulses, passivity of volition, auditory hallucinations that described actions as they took place, hallucinatory voices discussing the patient, and primary delusions (see Appendix). Thirty-eight had one or more "first rank" symptoms. The details are in Table II.

The change in clinical state was rated on a scale from −1 to 4: −1) worse, 0) unchanged, 1) minimal improvement, 2) moderate improvement, 3) marked improvement, and 4) complete remission. The scale for rating the severity of toxic effects was: 0) none; 1) mild, not interfering with the patient significantly; 2) moderate, interfering with the patient significantly; and 3) severe.

TABLE I. Details of Illness, Previous Treatment, and Remission

					Previous treatment			
Case no.	Sex	Age at onset	No. of episodes	Yr. of remission	chlorpromazine, mg/day	trifluoperazine, mg/day	fluphenazine decanoate mg/2 wks	haloperidol, mg/day
1	M	23	1	0	800	30		
2	M	23	2	4	300			
3	F	24	1	0	400			
4	M	33	1	0	800	15	12	05
5	F	25	2	3	800	15		15
6	M	19	1	0	450		25	
7	M	18	1	0	150		25	
8	F	27	1	0	100	15	12.5	05
9	F	13	1	0	300		25	
10	M	27	1	0	400	10		
11	M	21	2	12	550		25	
12	F	26	3	4	900	15	37.5	15
13	M	26	1	0	250			
14	M	15	1	0	150		25	10
15	M	20	1	0	1,000	30		
16	M	21	1	0	1,200	30		
17	M	24	1	0	1,000			
18	F	19	1	0	900	15	25	45
19	F	30	1	0		45		26
20	M	36	1	0	300			
21	F	45	1	0	400	30	25	7.5
22	M	18	1	0	300			
23	M	20	1	0	1,200	15	25	30
24	M	35	1	0	300			
25	F	54	1	0	300		25	
26	F	30	2	6	300	15		
27	M	24	1	0	300			
28	F	40	1	0		30		
29	M	30	1	0	300	35	25	
30	F	17	1	0	400			
31	M	31	1	0				
32	F	30	1	0	600	30		
33	M	25	3	5		15		
34	F	34	1	0	400	30	25	
35	M	60	1	0				
36	M	26	1	0	300	15		
37	M	19	1	0	800	15	25	
38	M	64	1	0				
39	M	24	1	0	250	15	25	
40	F	18	1	0	1,200		25	24
41	F	41	1	0				
42	F	22	4	10	400	15		
43	M	71	1	0				
44	M	22	1	0	100		25	15
45	F	25	2	3	300	15		
46	M	32	1	0				
47	F	23	1	0				
48	M	19	1	0	400			25
49	F	39	1	0		15	25	
50	F	18	1	0	150			
51	M	25	1	0				
52	M	19	1	0				
53	F	51	3	12	300			03
54	M	15	1	0		03	25	
55	F	28	1	0	150		12.5	

Age propranolol started (yr.)	Dosage at remission (concurrent drugs)				
	propranolol, mg/day	chlorpromazine, mg/day	trifluoperazine, mg/day	fluphenazine decanoate mg/2 wks	haloperidol, mg/day
24	2,000		15		
30	1,500		30		
24	3,000				
39	1,500				
43			30		
25	2,500				
31		400			
36			20		
20			30		
48					
33	500				
35			20	25	
28	1,250				
22	2,500				
35					
48		150			
47			15		
28			20	25	
41	500				
37	500				
56					
18	1,500				
25					10
35	1,375				
72			10		
42			15		
29					
40					
35				25	
24					
31	1,250				
44			15		
35					
62	1,240		15		
61					
27	1,000				
28				12.5	
64	500				
46	820		15		
39					
45					
39	790		15		
71	1,250				
22	500				
45	160		15		
34					
23	1,250				
27	750		20		
52	640			25	
30	580		15		
25	500				
21	660				
76			10		
22			10		
29	160				

TABLE II. "First Rank" Symptoms of Schizophrenia

	Total	Case number														Case number													
Symptom	(of 53)	1	2	3	4	5	6	7	8	9	10	11	12	13	14	15	16	17	18	19	20	21	22	23	24	25	26	27	28
Primary delusion	3	—	—	—	—	—	—	—	—	—			—	—	—			—	—	—	—	—	—	—	—	—	—	—	+
Passivity of volition	11	—	—	—	—	—	—	—	—	—			—	+	—			—	+	+	—	—	—	+	+	—	+	—	—
Passivity of feelings or impulses	11	—	—	—	—	—	+	—	—	+			—	+	+			—	+	+	—	—	—						
Audible thoughts	11	+	+	—	—	+	—	+	—	+			—	—	+			—	—	—	—	—	—	—	—	—	—	—	+
Somatic passivity	14	+	—	—	—	+	—	+	—	+			—	—	—			—	+	+	+	—	—	+	—	—	—	—	+
Thought withdrawal	15	+	+	—	—	+	—	+	+	+			—	—	+			—	—	—	+	—	—	—	+	—	—	—	—
Hallucinatory voices													—	—															
discussing patient	20	—	+	—	+	+	—	+	+	+			+	+	+			—	—	—	+	—	—	—	—	—	+	—	—
Auditory hallucinations describing actions	21	—	—	—	+	+	—	+	+	+			+	+	+			—	—	+	+	—	—	—	—	—	+	—	—
Thought broadcast	23	+	—	—	+	+	+	+	—	+			—	—	+			—	—	—	—	+	+	—	+	—	+	+	—
Thought insertion	24	+	+	—	+	+	+	+	+	+			+	—	+			—	—	—	+	+	—	+	+	—	+	—	+
Total (of 53)		5	4	0	4	8	2	7	4	8		0	3	4	7	0	0	0	3	4	5	2	1	3	4	0	6	2	4

TABLE II. continued

Symptoms	Total (of 53)	Case number 29	30	31	32	33	34	35	36	37	38	39	40	41	42	Case number 43	44	45	46	47	48	49	50	51	52	53	54
Primary delusion	3	−	+	−	−	−	+	−	−	−	−	−		−	−	−	−	−	−	−	−	−	−	−	−		−
Passivity of volition	11	+	−	−	−	−	+	−	−	−	−	−		−	−	−	+	−	−	+	−	−	−	−	−		−
Passivity of feelings or impulses	11	+	−	−	−	−	−	−	−	−	−	−		−	−	−	−	−	−	−	−	−	−	−	+		−
Audible thoughts	11	−	+	−	−	−	−	−	+	−	−	−		−	−	−	−	−	−	−	−	−	−	−	−		+
Somatic passivity	14	+	+	−	−	−	+	−	−	−	−	−		−	−	−	−	−	−	−	−	−	+	+	−		−
Thought withdrawal	15	+	−	−	−	−	+	−	−	−	−	−		−	−	−	+	−	−	−	−	−	+		+		−
Hallucinatory voices discussing patient	20		+	+	−	−	+	−	+	+	−	−		−	+	−	−	−	−	−	−	−	+		−		+
Auditory hallucinations describing actions	21	+	+	+	−	−	+	−	+	+	−	−		−	+	−	−	−	−	−	−	−	+	−	−		+
Thought broadcast	23	+	−	−	+	−	+	−	−	−	−	−		−	−	−	+	+	−	+	−	+	+	+	+		−
Thought insertion	24	+	−	+	+	−	+	−	−	−	−	−		−	−	−	+	+	−	−	−	−	−	−	+		−
Total (of 53)		7	5	3	2	0	8	0	3	2	0	0		0	2	0	4	2	0	2	0	1	5	2	4	0	3

Dosage

Propranolol was given alone, or combined with a phenothiazine drug (6, 7). The policy was to alter one main variable at a time. At first, propranolol was given to patients who had not responded to phenothiazine drugs. Gradually, propranolol came to be given as the first drug because some patients responded quickly and none developed extrapyramidal symptoms or signs.

A low dose was usually ineffective. Too high a dose, particularly when reached quickly by increments of 400–800 mg/day (1), was likely to give acute toxic effects, such as slurred speech and ataxia (2). Practical safeguards included daily observations and raising the dose in steps of 40–80 mg/day (6, 7). Regular dosage, for example, twice every day, seemed necessary to produce a smooth therapeutic response. Experience in noticing both early signs of improvement and early signs of toxicity was valuable in learning to regulate the dose.

RESULTS

Therapeutic Effects

All schizophrenic symptoms remitted, at least temporarily, in 28 out of the 55 patients (Table III).

Seventeen of the patients whose symptoms remitted were taking propranolol alone. (These are indicated by the numbers in parentheses in Table III. See also Figs. 1 and 2). Eleven patients whose symptoms remitted were taking propranolol combined with a phenothiazine drug. This was often trifluoperazine which seemed less likely to cause drowsiness or hypotension than chlorpromazine when combined with propranolol.

Better results were obtained in those who had been ill for less than one year. Symptoms also remitted, however, in some very long-standing illnesses. For example, when propranolol was added to phenothiazine treatment, schizophrenic symptoms slowly remitted in two patients who had been ill for

TABLE III. Outcome, Grouped by Duration of Episode*

Outcome rating	Duration of episode (years)					
	under 1	1–5	6–10	11–20	21–30	Total
Worse	0	0	0	0	0	0
Unchanged	0	0	1(0)	0	0	1(0)
Improved minimally	0	1(0)	1(0)	2(2)	1(0)	5(2)
Improved moderately	1(1)	1(1)	3(0)	2(1)	1(0)	8(3)
Improved markedly	3(2)	2(1)	4(3)	3(1)	1(0)	13(7)
Remitted completely	13(10)	6(4)	4(2)	3(1)	2(0)	28(17)
Total	17(13)	10(6)	13(5)	10(5)	5(0)	55(29)

*Patients treated with propranolol alone are shown in parentheses. The rest had propranolol added to a phenothiazine drug.

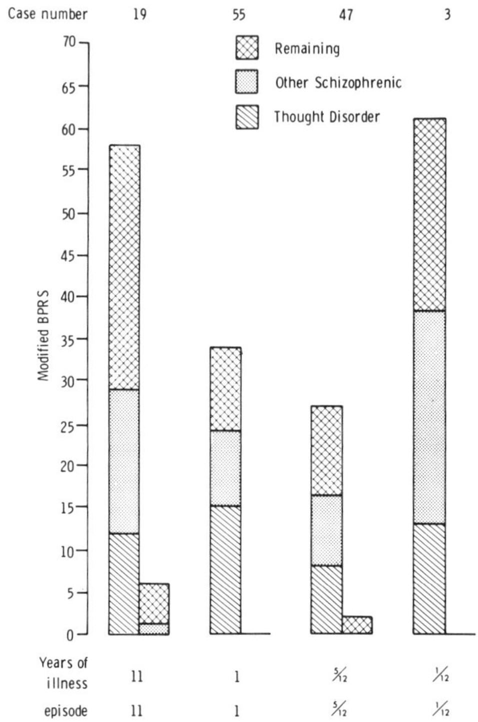

Fig. 1. Modified BPRS scores for the four women whose symptoms remitted on propranolol alone, without being combined with phenothiazine drugs. The pairs of ratings are those made before propranolol was started and at the last rating before the time of writing.

more than twenty years. Table III shows that schizophrenic symptoms remitted in 13 out 17 (76%) of those whose current episode of illness had lasted for less than one year, and in 19 out of 27 (70%) patients whose episode was of less than five years' duration (Table III). Nine out of twenty-eight patients whose current episode had lasted longer than five years also lost their schizophrenic symptoms. The results for the individual patients are shown in Figures 1–6.

Remissions on propranolol. The format used in Figures 1–6 may be seen clearly in Figure 1. This summarizes the clinical progress of the four women whose schizophrenic symptoms disappeared while taking propranolol alone, without it being

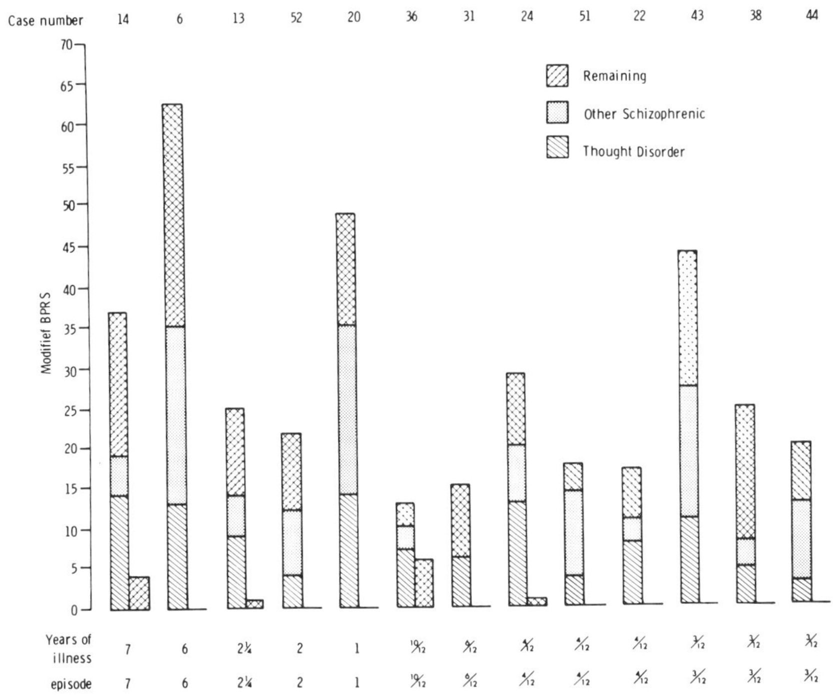

Fig. 2. Modified BPRS scores for the 13 men whose symptoms remitted on propranolol alone, without concurrent phenothiazine drugs.

combined with a phenothiazine drug. The histograms illustrate two ratings for each patient on the modified BPRS. The left rating was made before propranolol was started and the right was the last rating made before the time of writing. The interval between these ratings varied widely because the individual follow-up time for the patients whose symptoms remitted varied from ten days to nearly two years. The vertical columns of the histogram are divided into three parts. The lower single-hatched portion represents the "thought disorder" scores. It may be recalled that a minimum score of three ("moderate") was required for a patient to enter this study. The middle, stippled section represents the total of the "other schizophrenia" scores – otherwise called the "non-thought disorder schizophrenia" scores (10). To enter this study, it will be recalled, a patient required a "total schizophrenia" score of at least six, comprised of at least three points from two different scales. The cross-hatched section at the top of the histogram represents the total score on the "remaining" scales – otherwise called the "nonschizophrenia" scales (10).

The number of years from the first onset of clearly psychotic symptoms to the time propranolol was started is shown for each patient as the "years of illness" (11). The duration of the current episode of illness, as defined above (11), before propranolol was given is also shown. In the cases of the four women illustrated in Figure 1 the episode of illness treated with propranolol was in each case the first episode. The individual case number (1–55) is shown.

Figure 1 thus summarizes the clinical progress of the four women whose schizophrenic symptoms disappeared when taking propranolol alone without a concomitant phenothiazine drug. They include the third and the last (55th) case from this series. All originally had much higher "total schizophrenia" scores than were required to enter the study. The duration of their illnesses varied from the shortest in this series (five weeks) to eleven years. The clinical judgement that their schizophrenic symptoms had remitted is reflected in the modified BPRS "schizophrenia" ratings which fell to zero in three cases. In the case of patient 19, however, "hostility" was rated as very mild. In the whole series several patients had low scores for the "remaining" or "non-schizophrenia" scales. For example, some had low scores for anxiety over taking tablets, their jobs, or other practical responsibilities. In all patients whose symptoms were thought to have remitted the "thought disorder" scales fell to zero.

The data for the 13 men whose symptoms remitted with propranolol alone, without an accompanying phenothiazine drug, are given in Figure 2. All these patients originally had much higher scores than the minimum required to enter the study. The episode of illness had continued for less than six months in six patients, less than one year in eight patients, and from one to seven years in five patients.

There was no case of paranoid schizophrenia with a chronic, systematized delusional state among the 17 patients who lost all their schizophrenic symptoms with propranolol alone.

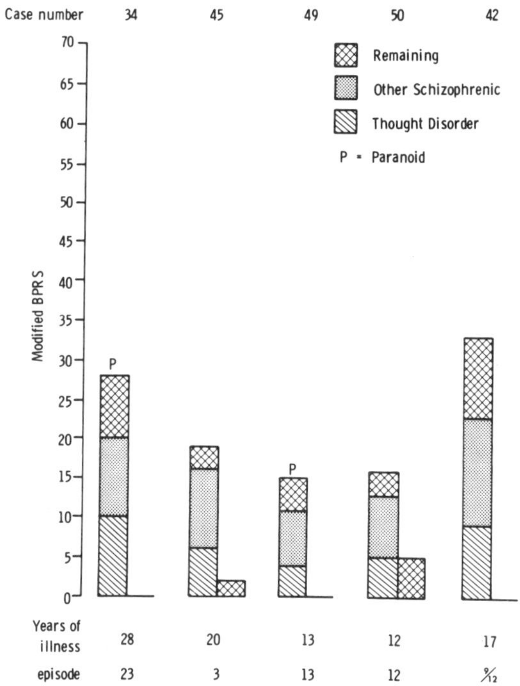

Fig. 3. Modified BPRS scores for the five women whose symptoms remitted with propranolol combined with a phenothiazine drug.

Remission on phenothiazines and propranolol. The progress of five women and six men who lost their schizophrenic symptoms when on propranolol and a phenothiazine drug together are represented in Figures 3 and 4. Their initial scores were also well above the total required to enter the study. Of these 11 patients, 9 had been ill for one year or more, 6 had been ill for over five years, and 2 for more than twenty years. Three patients had a paranoid illness characterized by a chronic, systematized delusional state.

Patients whose symptoms did not remit. In half the patients (27 out of 55) the symptoms of schizophrenia had not remitted by the time of writing. Table III shows that no patient in this group was rated as worse, one was unchanged, and the

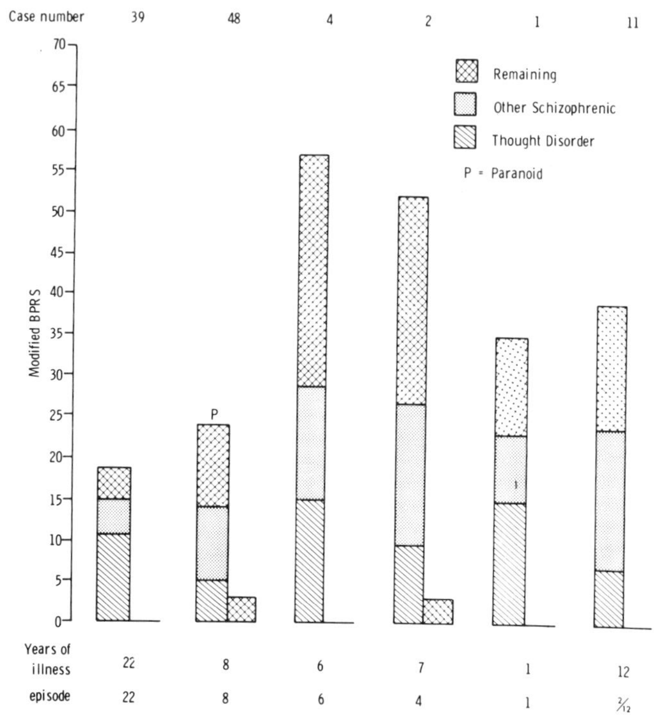

Fig. 4. Modified BPRS scores for the six men whose symptoms remitted with propranolol combined with a phenothiazine drug.

rest were rated in varying grades of improvement. Five were rated as minimally improved, 8 as moderately improved, and 13 as markedly improved. The 14 women and 13 men who did not lose all their schizophrenic symptoms are represented in Figures 5 and 6. Patient 21 (in Fig. 5) had improved with propranolol, but deteriorated when she refused to continue it. Of the 27 patients, 23 were treated for an episode which had lasted for more than two years, 10 had a chronic, systematized delusional state and were thus diagnosed as having a paranoid illness, and 12 had not taken propranolol combined with a phenothiazine drug.

Chronicity. The duration of the episodes of illness (11) in which the symptoms remitted varied from five weeks in the

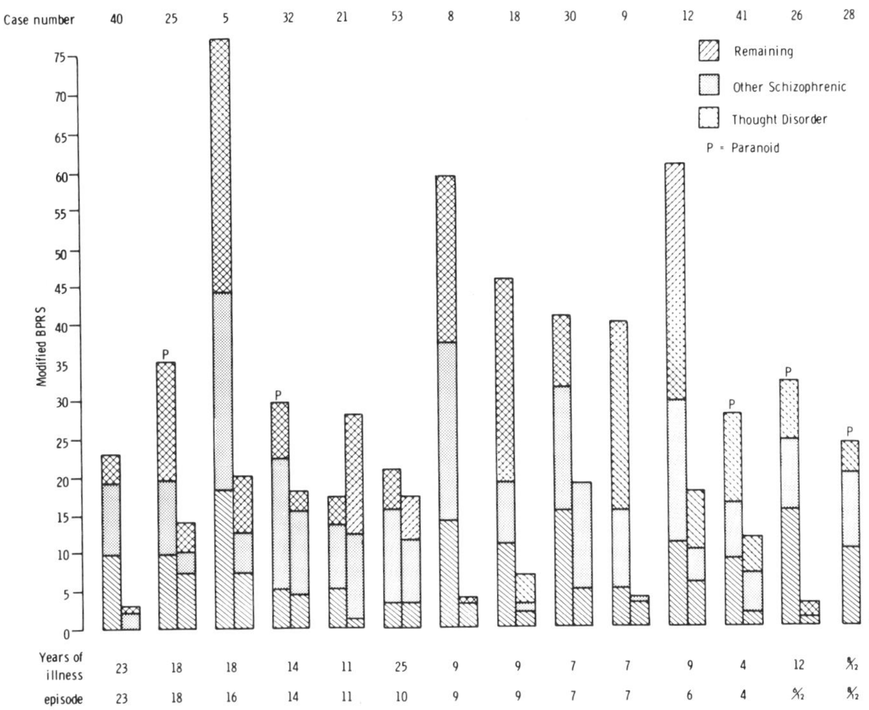

Fig. 5. Modified BPRS scores for the 14 women who did not lose all their schizophrenic symptoms. ? indicates that no recent rating was available.

case of a woman with puerperal psychosis (*case 3*) to 22 and 23 years (*cases 34* and *39*) in two patients with hebephrenic and paranoid schizophrenia.

The total duration of illness (11) in the patients whose symptoms remitted varied from five weeks (*case 3*) to 28 years (*case 34*). The lengths of the episode and illness for each patient are given in Figures 1–6.

Pattern of recovery. The pattern of recovery was usually gradual. Careful observation at first was needed to detect the early, slight but definite signs of improvement in patients whose grossly psychotic behavior was only too plain (6, 7). They became calmer and less irritable, developed better eye contact and more coherent speech, gradually lost their

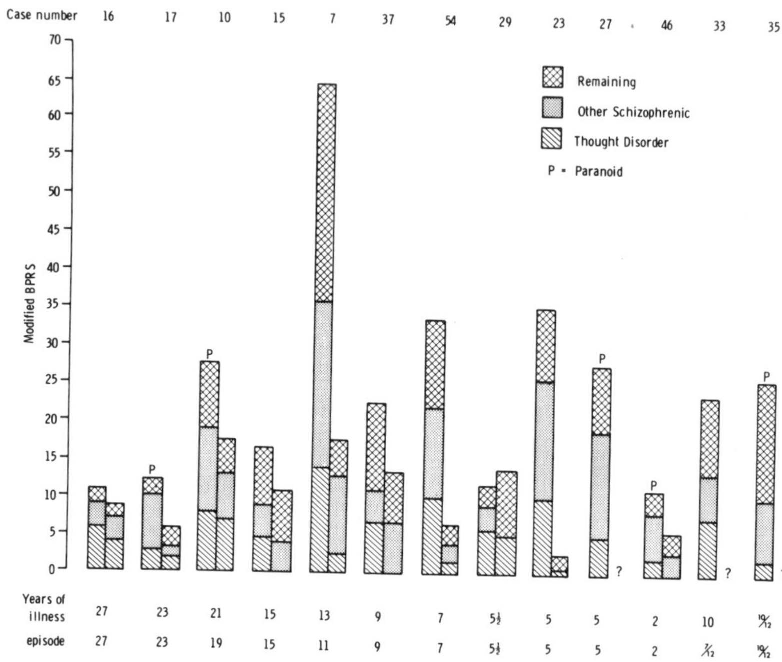

Fig. 6. Modified BPRS scores for the 13 men who did not lose all their schizophrenic symptoms. ? indicates that no recent rating was available.

hallucinations, distorted perceptions, and ideas of reference, and finally, after many weeks, secondary delusions remitted.

In 6 out of 28 of the patients in whom the schizophrenic symptoms remitted, the symptoms stopped suddenly. Five patients identified the day on which their hallucinations stopped (*cases 1, 4, 6, 36,* and *42*). The sixth could point to the chair on which she was sitting when "my mind clicked back" (*case 50*).

Improvement and remission usually seemed to be related to propranolol, given either alone or combined with a phenothiazine drug. Symptoms returned within 72 hours in nearly every patient who stopped taking propranolol (6, 7).

In all 28 patients whose symptoms remitted the "thought disorder" scores fell to zero. For practical purposes all the "other schizophrenia" scores also fell to zero. (Patient 19, as noted above, was rated as "very mild" for hostility.)

Paranoid patients with a chronic, systematized delusional state seemed the most difficult to treat. Even when their ideas of reference stopped, the delusional systems still held firm. Often at this stage of partial improvement they asserted that they were perfectly well and discontinued treatment. All schizophrenic symptoms remitted in only 3 out of the 13 paranoid patients (Table IV). *Cases 34* and *48* received propranolol combined with trifluoperazine and *case 49* had two injections of fluphenazine decanoate.

Schizophrenic symptoms remitted in 25 out of 42 patients (60%) who did not have a chronic, systematized delusional state and who were therefore classified as having a nonparanoid illness. These comprised one patient with puerperal psychosis (*case 3*), four out of five patients with schizoaffective psychosis, and 20 out 36 (55%) patients with hebephrenic schizophrenia.

Dose. The dose of propranolol required for remission of schizophrenic symptoms varied widely. In the 17 patients who lost their symptoms with propranolol alone, the dose associated with remission ranged from 160 to 3,000 mg/24 hr, with the median being 1,250 mg/24 hr. Figure 7 shows the individual remission doses. The maintenance dose ranged from 160 to 2,000 mg/24 hr, with the median being 500 mg/24 hr.

Figure 8 shows the dose of propranolol at remission for the 11 patients who lost their schizophrenic symptoms when on both propranolol and a phenothiazine drug. The propranolol dose range was 160 to 2,000 mg/24 hr, and the median dose was 820 mg/24 hr. The maintenance dose ranged from 160 to 1,500 mg/24 hr (median 750 mg/24 hr).

TABLE IV. Outcome, Grouped by Diagnosis

	Paranoid	Nonparanoid hebephrenic	Nonparanoid schizo-affective	Nonparanoid puerperal	Total
Male	6	22	4	0	32
Female	7	14	1	1	23
Total	13	36	5	1	55
Remissions	3/13	20/36	4/5	1/1	28/55

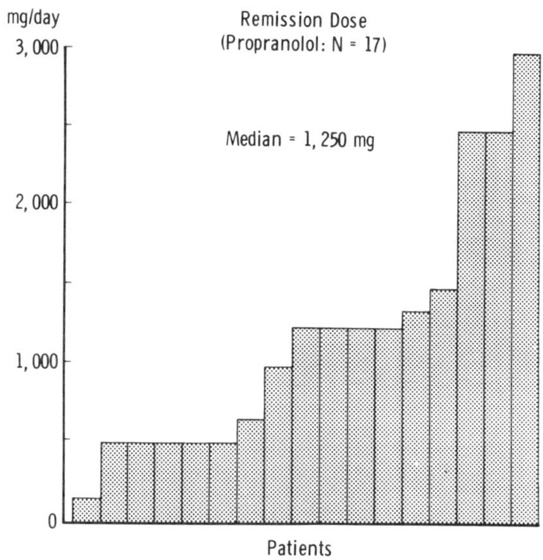

Fig. 7. Dose of propranolol at remission in 17 patients who were not also taking a phenothiazine drug.

Time to remission. The time from starting propranolol to the remission of schizophrenic symptoms varied from three days (*case 6*) to one year (*case 14*). Figure 9 shows the relationship of the weeks on propranolol to the time of remission in the 17 patients who lost their schizophrenic symptoms with propranolol alone. These intervals ranged from 72 hours to one year, and the median was eight weeks.

Figure 10 shows the number of weeks from starting propranolol to remission in the 11 patients who lost their schizophrenic symptoms while taking both propranolol and a phenothiazine drug. The time varied from 9 to 52 weeks, and the median was 34 weeks.

Table V summarizes the time on propranolol and the dosage for the 28 patients whose symptoms remitted.

Follow-up. Follow-up of this uncontrolled study is not complete. The follow-up interval from remissions to the time of this survey varied from 10 days (*case 50*) to 20 months (*cases 3* and *6*).

Toxic Effects

Acute. For practical purposes all the toxic effects were acute, and subsided within hours after propranolol was withheld. Most of the severe effects occurred early in this series. Later, toxic effects were less frequent, and when they occurred were usually moderate or mild (Table VI). They occurred most often when the dose was raised quickly, by 400–800 mg/24 hr, when propranolol was given four or more times in

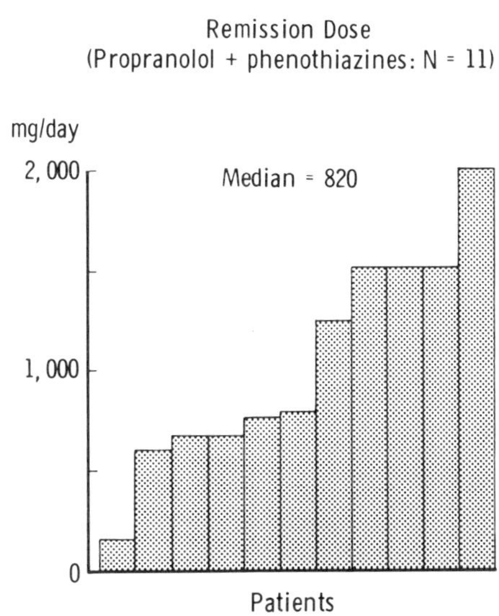

Fig. 8. Dose of propranolol at remission in 11 patients who were taking it with a phenothiazine drug.

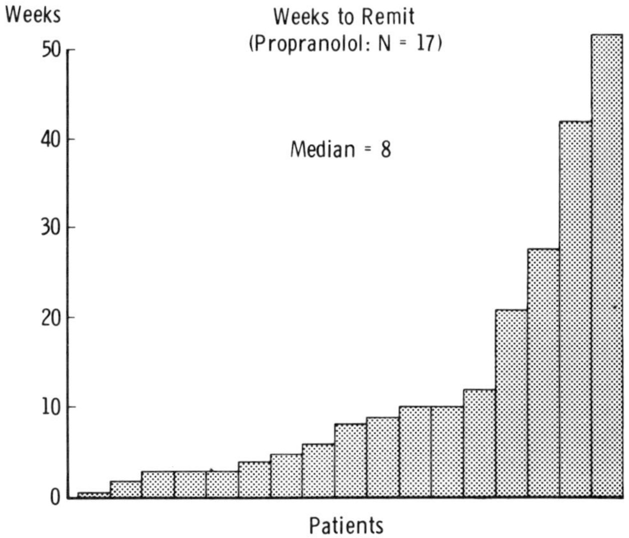

Fig. 9. Time (weeks) from starting propranolol to remission of symptoms in 17 patients who were not also taking a phenothiazine drug.

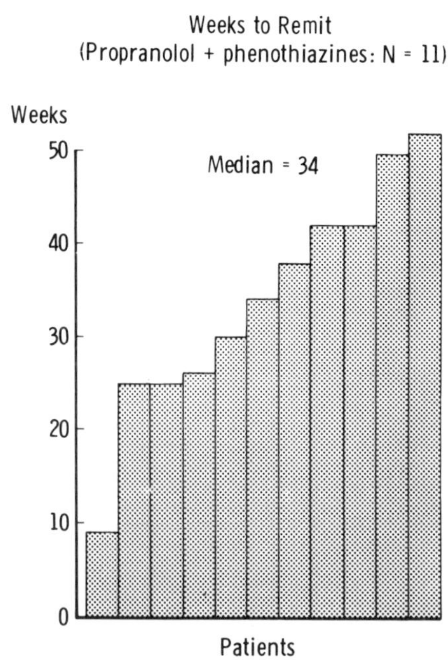

Fig. 10. Time (weeks) from starting propranolol to remission of symptoms in 11 patients who were taking it with a phenothiazine drug.

TABLE V. Remissions: Time and Dosage of Propranolol

		Weeks to remission		Remission dose (mg/24 hr)		Maintenance dose (mg/24 hr)	
	Number	median	range	median	range	median	range
Propranolol	17	8	0.5–52	1,250	160–3,000	500	160–2,000
Propranolol + phenothiazines	11	34	9 –52	820	160–2,000	750	160–1,500
Total	28	17	0.5–52	1,125	160–3,000	500	160–2,000

TABLE VI. Acute Toxic Effects: Incidence and Severity in 23 Cases*

	Case number											
	1	2	3	4	5	7	8	9	16	17	18	19
Ataxia	+	+	+	+	+	+	+	+	+	+	+	+
Dysarthria	+	+	+	+	+	+	+	−	+	+	+	+
Falls	+	+	−	+	+	−	−	+	+	−	−	−
Pallor	+	+	−	+	−	+	−	+	−	−	+	−
Visual hallucinations	+	−	+	−	−	+	+	+	−	−	−	−
Confusional state	+	+	+	+	−	+	−	−	+	−	+	−
Overactive	−	+	+	+	+	−	−	−	+	−	+	−
Hysterical behavior	−	−	+	+	−	+	−	−	+	−	−	−
Nausea	−	−	−	+	−	−	−	+	−	−	−	+
Cardiovascular	+	−	−	+	−	−	−	−	−	+	−	−
Faint	+	−	−	−	−	−	−	−	−	−	−	−
Severity	3	3	2	2	2	2	1	1	3	2	2	2

TABLE VI. continued

	Case number											
	26	27	29	34	36	39	40	42	43	45	46	Total
Ataxia	+	+	+	+	−	+	−	−	−	+	+	19
Dysarthria	+	+	+	−	−	+	−	+	−	+	−	17
Falls	−	+	−	+	−	−	−	−	−	−	−	8
Pallor	−	−	−	−	−	+	−	−	−	−	−	7
Visual hallucinations	−	−	−	−	+	−	−	−	−	−	+	7
Confusional state	−	+	+	−	−	−	−	−	−	−	−	9
Overactive	−	+	+	−	−	−	−	−	−	−	−	8
Hysterical behavior	−	+	+	−	−	−	−	−	−	+	−	7
Nausea	+	−	−	−	−	−	−	−	−	−	+	5
Cardiovascular	−	−	−	−	−	−	−	−	+	−	−	4
Faint	−	+	−	−	−	−	+	+	−	−	−	4
Severity	1	3	3	2	1	1	1	1	2	1	1	

*The other 32 patients had no toxic effects. No chronic toxic effects were seen.

24 hours, or if after missing several doses the drug was resumed at the same dose. The acute toxic effects, with the safeguards to avoid and to treat them, have been described (6, 7). Thirty-two patients had no toxic effects. Nine had mild toxic effects which were not troublesome, nine had moderate toxic effects which temporarily inconvenienced them, and five patients had severe short-term toxic effects that subsided in a few hours.

The most common toxic effect was incoordination. Out of the 23 who had toxic effects 19 had ataxia, 17 showed dysarthria, and 8 had falls (Table VI). Pallor of the lips and ears, visual hallucinations, and a confusional state sometimes occurred. A changed pattern of abnormal behavior, such as becoming overactive or behaving hysterically, were also probably toxic symptoms (6, 7).

Nausea was usually avoided by taking the tablets after meals. Four people had cardiovascular effects: One had a transient rise in blood pressure (*case 1*) (2), one possibly had angina (*case 4*), one had a myocardial infarction which may or may not have been coincidental (*case 17*), and one had cardiac failure which responded to standard treatment (*case 43*). The lowered pulse and blood pressure were not included in this list as they were symptomless and served to guide the dosage (6, 7). Toxic effects often occurred together (Table VI), but subsided within hours when propranolol was withheld and the patient rested.

Subacute. The nearest approach to any chronic toxic effect that occasionally was observed was the following sequence of events. When a period of irregular dosage was followed for some days by steady dosage, patients sometimes became agitated, but calmed down again when the dose was reduced. We were inclined to interpret this as a subacute toxic effect.

Chronic. No long-term toxic effects were seen.

DISCUSSION

Propranolol is believed to control schizophrenic symptoms not only because these symptoms often improved after starting the drug, but particularly because the symptoms often recurred within one to three days after a patient whose symptoms had remitted stopped taking propranolol. In cases of relapse it seemed distinctly more difficult to treat the recurrence than to achieve the first remission. Symptoms which remitted for ten days in one patient, who then stopped taking her tablets, returned and did not remit again in spite of repeated attempts over a period of more than a year. We therefore think that a patient whose symptoms remit with propranolol should not be taken off the drug for a cross-over study.

Remissions of schizophrenic symptoms gave a definite standard by which to assess the response to treatment. Intermediary points on the outcome scale were less definite because they depended on clinical estimates. Of course, remission was not an end-point in the sense of producing a cure. Relapse almost invariably followed stopping propranolol.

Modifying the BPRS to score from 0 to 6 (2) (instead of from 1 to 7)(9) helped to illustrate remission because the "schizophrenia" scores fell to zero.

The fact that toxic effects became progressively less common through this series suggests that experience in monitoring the patients' progress gave a better guide to dosage. Plainly it is desirable to prevent toxic effects to avoid unpleasant or even dangerous experiences for the patient. Furthermore, some patients who had a toxic reaction became extremely averse to taking propranolol, and they were turned against a drug which might, and in some cases apparently did, later effect a remission. Toxic reactions were also long remembered by the staff, sometimes more vividly than the remissions.

To report progress at this stage means describing incomplete work. For example, 12 out of the 27 patients whose symptoms did not remit have not taken propranolol in combination with a phenothiazine drug. The follow-up is short and still incomplete. Further analyses of the data from this uncontrolled study may give further information.

Schizophrenia research has been notoriously "littered with false dawns" (13). The British Medical Journal commented that propranolol for schizophrenia "could be an important discovery, or simply another treatment to add to the long list that time has shown to be inefficacious" (14). The latter article looked forward to the results of controlled studies.

An "instant controlled study" (15) was contraindicated until the clinical team learned to use the drug in its new setting and developed safeguards for its use (6, 7). However, this uncontrolled study has prepared the way for current controlled studies, and the first of these showed that propranolol significantly helped chronic schizophrenic patients whose florid symptoms had not remitted with major tranquillizers (10).

ACKNOWLEDGMENTS

We thank the editors of Advances in Clinical Pharmacology and of Neuro-Psychiatric Effects of Adrenergic Beta-Receptor Blocking Agents for permission to reproduce some data previously published.

REFERENCES

1. Atsmon A: Personal communication, 1972.
2. Yorkston NJ, Zaki SA, Malik MKU, Morrison RC, Havard CWH: Propranolol in the control of schizophrenic symptoms. Br Med J 4:633–635, 1974.
3. Yorkston NJ: Beta-adrenergic blockade in the control of schizophrenic symptoms: a case for controlled studies. Scot Med J 20: 292–294, 1975.
4. Steiner M, Blum I, Wijsenbeek H, Atsmon A: Results of the treatment of psychoses with propranolol. Kupat Holim Yearbook 2: 201–209, 1972.
5. Atsmon A: Early observations of the effect of propranolol on psychotic patients. Adv Clin Pharmacol 12:86–90, 1976.
6. Yorkston NJ, Zaki SA, Themen JFA, Havard CWH: Safeguards in the treatment of schizophrenia with propranolol. Postgrad Med J 52(Suppl 4):175–180, 1976.
7. Yorkston NJ, Zaki SA, Havard CWH: Some practical aspects of using propranolol in the treatment of schizophrenia. This volume, pp 83–97.

8. Turner WJ: "Glossaries for Use with the Overall and Gorham Brief Psychiatric Rating Scale and for a Modified Malamud-Sands Rating Scale." Research Division, Central Islip State Hospital, Central Islip, New York, 1963.
9. Overall JE, Gorham DR: The brief psychiatric rating scale. Psychol Rep 10:799–812, 1962.
10. Yorkston NJ, Gruzelier JH, Zaki SA, Hollander D, Pitcher DR, Sergeant HGS: Propranolol as an adjunct to the treatment of schizophrenia. Lancet ii:575–578, 1977.
11. May PRA: "Treatment of Schizophrenia: A Comparative Study of Five Treatment Methods." New York: Science House, Inc., 1968.
12. Mellor CS: First rank symptoms of schizophrenia: I. The frequency in schizophrenics on admission to hospital. II. Differences between individual first rank symptoms. Br J Psychiatry 117:15–23, 1970.
13. Anonymous: Dimethyltryptamine and psychosis. Lancet ii:140–141, 1974.
14. Anonymous: New drug for schizophrenia? Br Med J 4:614, 1974.
15. Prichard BNC: In "Ten Years of Propranolol: A Symposium on the History and the Future of Beta-Blockade." 1976.

APPENDIX

Questionnaire for "First Rank" Symptoms

1. **Audible thoughts:**
   - Do you ever seem to hear your thoughts spoken aloud? (almost as if someone nearby could hear them) yes. . . . no. . . .
   - Do they repeat something you have just thought? yes. . . . no. . . .
   - Do they sometimes repeat the same sentence many times? yes. . . . no. . . .
2. **Somatic passivity:**
   - Do you ever feel that someone or something is touching you but when you look there is nobody there? Or as if there was something creeping under your skin? Or as if your skin was wet? yes. . . . no. . . .
   - Did you have any unusual or strange sexual sensations lately? What did you feel? When was that? How do you explain it? yes. . . . no. . . .
3. **Thought insertion:**
   - Are thoughts put into your mind which you know are not your own? Thoughts from elsewhere? How can you tell they are not yours? Who put them there? yes. . . . no. . . .
   - Is there a difference between your own thoughts and the other thoughts which have been put into your mind? yes. . . . no. . . .
4. **Thought withdrawal:**
   - Do you ever feel as if your thoughts were being taken away, so that your mind is a complete blank? Can you describe it? yes. . . . no. . . .

5. Thought broadcast:

- Do you feel that your thoughts are being broadcast, transmitted so that everyone knows what you are thinking? Can you describe this? yes. . . . no. . . .

6. Passivity of feelings or impulses:

- Do you ever feel that you are made to want things that you do not want yourself? yes. . . . no. . . .

7. Passivity of volition:

- Does some other force than you yourself make you do or say things that you do not intend? As though you were a robot without a will of your own? yes. . . . no. . . .
- Is someone else (or something) making your movements and actions for you without your intention? yes. . . . no. . . .
- What about your handwriting: is that controlled? yes. . . . no. . . .

8. Auditory hallucinations that comment:

- Do you hear a voice(s) describing your actions as they take place? yes. . . . no. . . .

9. Auditory hallucinations that converse:

- Do voices *talk* among themselves *about you*, discussing your actions or arguing over you? (patient usually referred to in the third person, e.g., Look what he is doing now!) yes. . . . no. . . .

10. Primary delusion:

- (This is a belief or feeling which arises de novo when some abnormal significance, usually with self reference, is attached to a genuine perception without any comprehensible, rational or emotional justification, e.g., a man spitting in the street indicates there is a plot to murder the patient. The delusion is not related to any affective state such as a depressive delusion would be.) yes. . . . no. . . .

3B. Propranolol as an Adjunct to the Treatment of Schizophrenia

Neil J. Yorkston, John H. Gruzelier, Saniha A. Zaki, Doris Hollander, David R. Pitcher, and Howard G. S. Sergeant

INTRODUCTION

Florid schizophrenic symptoms remitted, at least temporarily, in 28 out of 55 adults treated with propranolol in uncontrolled studies at Friern Hospital (1–4). The controlled study reported here was designed to compare the effects of adding either propranolol or a matching placebo to the treatment regimen of patients with chronic schizophrenia whose symptoms had not remitted with conventional treatment.

PATIENTS AND METHODS

Patients

Fourteen patients who had each been diagnosed by two psychiatrists as having chronic schizophrenia with florid symptoms and who could safely be given propranolol were selected for the trial. They were allotted at random to two groups, one group to receive propranolol, the other a placebo, for 12 weeks. The patients' average age was 40 years (range 27–55 years), the average age at onset of the illness was 30 years, and the current episode, which was usually the first, had

Propranolol and Schizophrenia, pages 69–82

lasted an average of nine years. The criteria of the Schizophrenic Research Project (5) were used to define the onset and duration of the illness. The patients had been treated for a mean of ten years with major tranquillizers. The average modal dose, expressed as the chlorpromazine equivalent (6), was 954 mg/day; the average maximum dose was 1,634 mg/day.

To be included in the study a patient had to be rated as "moderate" (at least) on two or more of the ten "schizophrenia" scales of a modified (1) Brief Psychiatric Rating Scale (BPRS) (7). At least one of these "moderate" ratings had to be on one of the three "thought disorder" scales – namely, conceptual disorganization, hallucinatory behavior, or unusual thought content. The seven "non-thought-disorder" schizophrenia scales were: blunted affect, emotional withdrawal, suspiciousness, grandiosity, mannerisms or posturing, hostility, and motor retardation. The sum of these ten "schizophrenia" scales gave the "total schizophrenia" score. There were also nine "non-schizophrenia" scales: somatic concern, anxiety, feelings of guilt, tension, depressed mood, uncooperativeness, excitement, disorientation, and pressure of speech.

"First rank" symptoms of schizophrenia (8) were looked for in a structured interview, and rated as not present if there was any doubt. The mean number for the sample was 3.6 out of a possible 10.

The diagnosis of schizophrenia was confirmed in all cases by trained raters using the Present State Examination (9). The Catego computer analysis (9) subclassified six patients in the propranolol group as paranoid and one as being in a paranoid state with unspecified psychosis. Five patients in the placebo group were subclassified as paranoid, one as being in a paranoid state with an unspecified psychosis, and one as either catatonic with psychomotor activity or in the manic phase of a manic-depressive illness.

Assessment

Independent consultant psychiatrists referred patients to the trial and reviewed them later. At four-weekly intervals ratings were made of symptoms (on the modified BPRS), the severity of illness (scale 0–6), and clinical change (scale 0–5).

The severity of illness was rated at the same intervals in answer to the question, "Considering your total clinical experience, how mentally ill is the patient now?". The ratings and their corresponding scores were: normal (0), borderline mentally ill (1), mildly (2), moderately (3), markedly (4), or severely (5) ill, or among the most extremely ill patients (6). Global ratings of change were made in reply to the question, "Compared to his condition at admission to the project, how much has he changed?" The possibilities were: worsened (5), unchanged (4), minimally (3), moderately (2), or markedly (1) improved, or completely remitted (0).

Nurses rated the patients' behavior on linear scales, scored from 0 to 10, before and at the end of the study. There were 24 items to be rated: slow movements, underactivity, overactivity, muteness, social isolation, leisure interests, talking to self, mannerisms or posturing, violence, incontinence, drug compliance, grooming, table manners, eye contact, staring, participation in ward life, incoherent speech, psychotic speech, courtesy, drowsiness, insomnia, occupation, eating, and well-being. Well-being, for example, was rated on a line between two extremes – "looks very well" and "looks very ill."

Treatment

During the 12-week trial the patients continued their previous medication and also had either propranolol or a placebo which looked and tasted the same.

After a test dose, propranolol (or placebo) was begun in a dose of 40 mg twice a day. The aim was to find the dose at which symptoms steadily improved (3). To this end patients were observed particularly for early signs of improvement and for early symptoms or signs of toxicity such as unsteadiness, slurred speech, or an excessive fall in pulse rate or blood pressure. Pulse rate and blood pressure were taken, with the patients seated, two hours after the morning dose. Lower limits were set for each patient – for example, a pulse rate of 60 beats per minute (sometimes 55 or 50) and a systolic blood pressure of 90 mm Hg. The dose was reviewed two or three times a week, and was raised by no more than 80 mg/day provided that there were no early toxic effects, and, secondly, that the symptoms of schizophrenia were *not* improving.

The doses of phenothiazines, thioxanthenes, or butyrophenones were expressed as equivalents of chlorpromazine (6). At the end of the study the daily dose, pulse rate, and blood pressure were summarized for each week by recording the highest and lowest levels and the mode (or the median, if there was no mode).

RESULTS

The groups before treatment were closely comparable (Table I). Table I shows the propranolol and placebo groups before treatment, giving their age, age at onset of schizophrenia, years in hospital, years free of illness, number of episodes, and length of the current episode. There were no statistically significant differences between the groups on any of these variables.

TABLE I. Groups Before Treatment

Variables	Propranolol (N = 7)	Placebo (N = 7)	value[a]
Sex (male:female)	3:4	2:5	
Age (mean)	39 years, 9 months	40 years, 9 months	0.24
Age of onset (mean)	32 years, 5 months	26 years, 7 months	1.42
Stay in hospital (mean)	4 years, 9 months	10 years, 7 months	1.68
Duration of remission (mean)	0.6 years	1.0 years	0.46
Number of episodes (mean)	1.3	1.9	0.75
Length of current episode (mean)	5 years, 11 months	11 years 6 months	1.37

[a] All nonsignificant.

Modified BPRS

Total schizophrenia scales. Before the trial the groups did not differ (Fig. 1). As the trial progressed the propranolol group improved significantly more ($F = 11.35$, df = 3, 36, $p < 0.001$) than the placebo group ($F = 3.06$, df = 3, 36, $p < 0.04$). Both groups improved significantly when the sum of the three thought-disorder scales were considered ($F = 17.2$, df = 3, 36, $p < 0.001$)(Table II). The propranolol group improved significantly more than the placebo group by week 12 ($F = 5.52$, df = 1, 12, $p < 0.035$). The non-thought-disorder schizophrenia scales (Table II) showed no difference at the beginning of the study ($F = 0.26$, df = 1, 12). By week 4 there was a tendency towards lower scores in the propranolol group, an effect which became progessively more significant between weeks 8 ($F = 4.62$, df = 1, 12, $p < 0.1$) and 12 ($F = 8.12$, df = 1, 11, $p < 0.03$).

Nonschizophrenia scales. No significant differences between the groups were found on the combined nonschizophrenia scales (Table II).

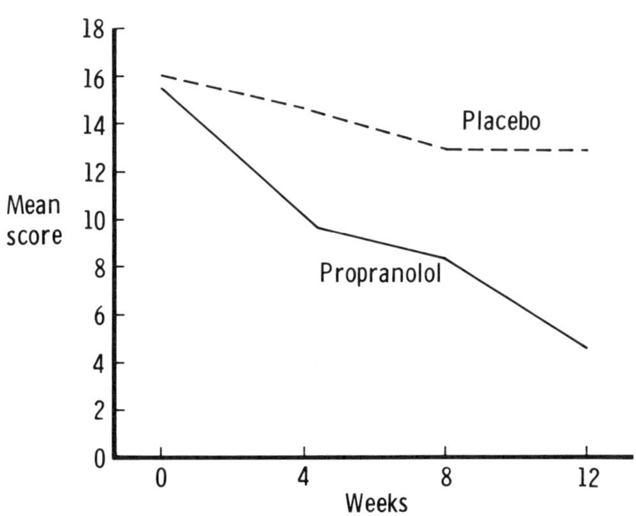

Fig. 1. Total "schizophrenia" scores (modified BPRS).

TABLE II. Modified BPRS Subscales and Ratings of Change and Severity of Illness (mean values)

	Week 0		Week 4		Week 8		Week 12	
	Propranolol	Placebo	Propranolol	Placebo	Propranolol	Placebo	Propranolol	Placebo
Thought disorder scales	9.9	9.4	6.4	7.3	5.0	6.0	2.6	6.3
Nonthought disorder scales	5.6	6.7	4.1	7.4	3.3	7.0	2.0	6.6
Nonschizophrenia scales	10.1	7.3	7.9	5.1	6.3	5.7	6.7	6.3
Global change	—	—	2.9	4.6	2.3	3.6	1.3	3.4
Severity of illness	4.4	4.6	3.6	4.4	2.7	3.6	2.0	3.7

Individual items. The only item that improved significantly more in the propranolol group was unusual thought content – delusions, and bizarre ideas ($F = 7.18$, df = 1, 12, $p < 0.05$). Two other items, grandiosity and conceptual disorganization, approached significance ($F = 3.20$, df = 1, 12, $p < 0.1$) and ($F = 3.96$, df = 1, 12, $p < 0.1$). Scores for these three items at the end of the trial were subtracted from those at the beginning. A discriminant function analysis was carried out to determine to what extent these items alone could differentiate between the groups. A significant discriminant was obtained ($\chi^2 = 10.10$, df = 3, $p = 0.018$) which correctly assigned all 14 patients to their appropriate group.

Psychiatrists' Ratings

By week 4 the global ratings of clinical change favored the propranolol group ($F = 3.57$, $p < 0.1$), and became significant by weeks 8 ($F = 6.30$, $p < 0.05$) and 12 ($F = 11.20$, $p < 0.005$) (Table II). Before the trial all 14 patients were rated as either very ill or severely ill, and there was no difference between the groups (Table II). When the trial ended the propranolol group (mean 2.0) was rated as significantly less ill than the placebo group (mean 3.7) ($F = 5.11$, df = 12, $p < 0.05$).

Nurses' Ratings

The groups were comparable before the study: the mean scores for the propranolol and placebo groups were 79.7 and 83.9, respectively. By week 12 the mean score (77.7) of the placebo group had not changed significantly ($F = 0.28$, df = 1, 12), but there was a highly significant improvement in the propranolol group – mean score 42.6 ($F = 10.11$, df = 1, 12, $p < 0.01$).

A change in the score was obtained for each item by subtracting the score at the end of the trial from that at the beginning. There were differences between the groups for three scales – well-being ($F = 9.63$, df = 1, 12, $p < 0.01$), incoherent speech ($F = 4.02$, df = 1, 12, $p < 0.01$), and violence ($F = 3.96$, df = 1, 12, $p < 0.01$).

Follow-up

After the 12th week, the code was broken. The seven patients in the propranolol group remained on the drug for an average follow-up period of 18.5 weeks and continued to improve. The two patients from this group who did not respond during the trial did so within the next month. Five patients in the placebo group were also given propranolol for an average of 15 weeks and improved significantly for the thought-disorder ($t = 4.10$, $df = 4$, $p < 0.01$) and non-thought-disorder ($t = 3.37$, $df = 4$, $p < 0.025$) schizophrenia scales.

At follow-up, 7 of the 12 who had received propranolol had lost all their florid schizophrenic symptoms. When the scores of the 12 patients who had been given propranolol were summated there were significant improvements for the thought-disorder scales ($t = 6.96$, $df = 11$, $p < 0.001$), the other schizophrenia scales ($t = 2.44$, $df = 11$, $p < 0.025$), and the nonschizophrenia scales ($t = 3.12$, $df = 11$, $p < 0.005$).

Consultants' Review

At follow-up, the 12 patients treated with propranolol were seen by their usual consultant psychiatrists. These eight psychiatrists rated the patients as "better than" (six patients), "as good as" (six patients), or "worse than" (no patient) the best they had known them to be before the trial.

Dose

The weekly modal doses of the experimental drugs were calculated for each patient. The group means for propranolol and placebo are shown in Figure 2. Doses were progressively increased in a similar manner for each group. None of the t tests carried out at weeks 4, 8, and 12 was significant (t values < 0.25).

There was no significant difference in the daily phenothiazine dose although it tended to be higher in the placebo group (mean 1,371 mg/day) than in the propranolol group (mean 972 mg/day), ($t = 0.92$, $df = 11$).

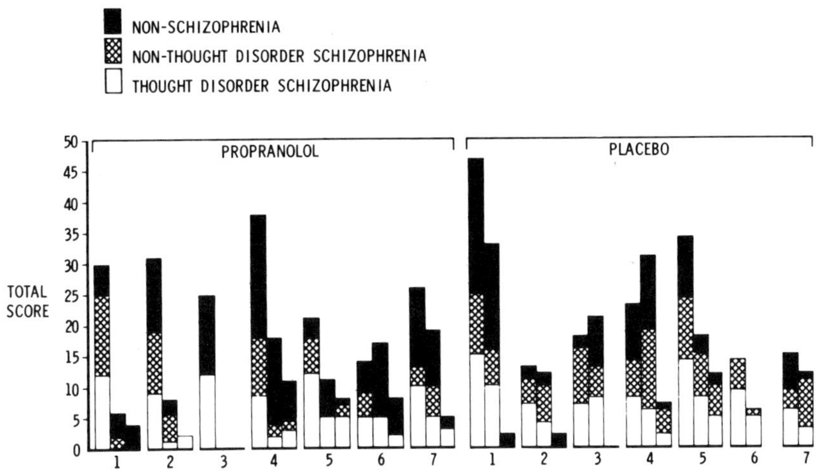

Fig. 2. Modified BPRS scores before the trial, at the end of the trial, and at follow-up for each patient. Patients 6 and 7 in the placebo group did not have propranolol.

Pulse Rate, Blood Pressure, and Toxicity

The groups did not differ in either pulse rate or blood pressure at the start of the trial. The weekly means for each group for the modal pulse rate and blood pressure are shown in Figure 3. There was a tendency for levels to be lower in the propranolol group than in the placebo group (Table III), but there was considerable overlap between groups in pulse rate (Fig. 4). There were no significant toxic effects. The trial code was broken before the 12th week (because of suspected side effects) for only one patient who was pale and had a low blood pressure. He was found to be on the placebo and the equivalent of 2,143 mg of chlorpromazine.

DISCUSSION

Propranolol contributed perceptibly to the treatment of chronic schizophrenia in patients who previously had not responded to major tranquillizers. The response of individual

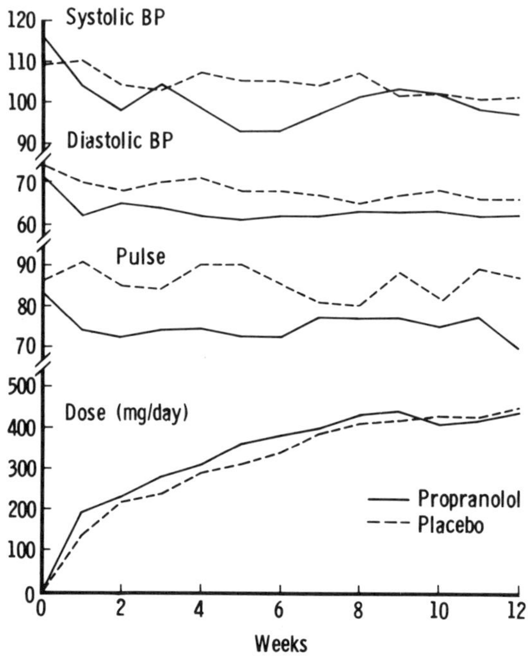

Fig. 3. Dose, pulse rate, and systolic and diastolic blood pressure for the propranolol and placebo groups.

TABLE III. Comparisons of Pulse and Blood Pressure at Weeks 0, 4, 8, and 12 (t test)

	Pulse		Systolic		Diastolic	
Week	t	p	t	p	t	p
0	0.47	ns	0.97	ns	0.23	ns
4	2.70	<0.01	0.70	ns	1.55	ns
8	0.57	ns	0.98	ns	0.64	ns
12	2.18	< 0.03	0.61	ns	1.07	ns

patients varied. Some had only a slight change in adjustment despite improved BPRS ratings and more coherent speech; others lost all their schizophrenic symptoms and were able to establish an independent life in the community.

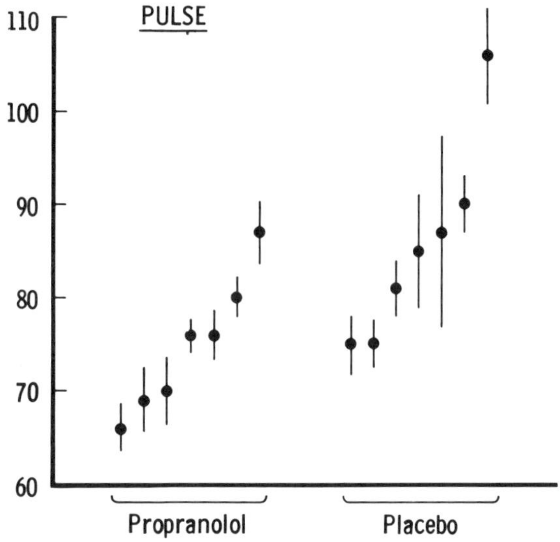

Fig. 4. Pulse rates: The mean and standard deviation for each patient are ranked according to the pulse rate.

In most cases the improvement was slow. It was not until the eighth week that differences were observed for the non-thought-disorder schizophrenia scales and not until the 12th week for the thought-disorder scales. Improvement continued after the 12-week trial, especially with the thought-disorder scales.

Facets of behavior not included in the BPRS also improved. The patients whose symptoms remitted often felt and looked well and relaxed, and spoke more fluently and naturally. These changes were reflected in the nurses' ratings where, for the item well-being, the difference between the groups was at a highly significant level.

The 12-week trial was probably too short to show the full effects of propranolol. In earlier studies the interval between starting the drug and remission varied from three days to one year (4), with a median of eight weeks for patients receiving propranolol alone, and 34 weeks when propranolol was combined with phenothiazines. The average dose of propranolol at the end of our trial (< 500 mg/day) was lower than the modal dose for remissions in earlier studies (4). It may reflect the reluctance of doctors to increase the dose in a double-blind trial.

Could there have been any bias in the ratings because they were made by people involved with the clinical treatment? One possible factor was the action of propranolol in reducing the pulse rate and blood pressure. But the fact that the doses of both propranolol and placebo were increased at virtually the same rate indicates that it would have been difficult to distinguish between the groups clinically.

All the patients showed some improvement. However, the personal attention they received cannot explain the difference in improvement between the groups.

How propranolol acts in schizophrenia is not known. However, it may be relevant that propranolol, which is lipid-soluble, readily passes the blood/brain barrier and is concentrated in the brain of animals (10–12) and man (12). Radioactively labeled propranolol given to rats is rapidly concentrated in the grey matter where it is retained, especially in the hippocampus (10). This may be connected with the finding that propranolol modulates the autonomic orienting reflex (13) – the reaction to a novel stimulus which Pavlov called the "what is it?" reflex (14). Limbic mechanisms may regulate orienting reactions (15). Schizophrenics usually show one of two abnormalities in their skin-conductance orienting reflexes: about half fail to orient (or orient only occasionally), and the half who do respond habituate slowly (16–20). Phenothiazine drugs rarely correct these abnormal orienting reactions. In contrast, propranolol, which has no effect on sweating, re-establishes a normal sequence of skin-conductance orienting responses in acute and chronic schizophrenics most of whom recover their ability to orient to novel sounds (70–90-dB tones) and to habituate normally when the tones are repeated (13). Propranolol may therefore have central effects on the complex processes of emotion and information. Neurophysiological measures such as these may eventually help in predicting the outcome of treatment.

ACKNOWLEDGMENTS

We thank the nursing staff at Friern Hospital for their invaluable help; Dr. J. J. Bradley, Dr. J. T. Bruce, Dr. J. R. W. Christie Brown, Dr. J. D. Hailstone, and Dr. R. A. Hunter for their assessments; Dr. H. A. Johnston for his advice; and I. C. I. Pharmaceuticals Division and the Sir Jules Thorn Medical Research Endowment Trust for grants towards this work. We also thank the editors of the Lancet for permission to reproduce, with some editorial changes, an article which appeared in the Lancet ii:575–578, 1977.

REFERENCES

1. Yorkston NJ, Zaki SA, Malik MKU, Morrison RC, Havard CWH: Propranolol in the control of schizophrenic symptoms. Br Med J 4:633–635, 1974.
2. Yorkston NJ: Beta-adrenergic blockade in the control of schizophrenic symptoms: a case for controlled studies. Scot Med J 20: 292–294, 1975.
3. Yorkston NJ, Zaki SA, Themen JFA, Havard CWH: Safeguards in the treatment of schizophrenia with propranolol. Postgrad Med J 52 (suppl 4):175–180, 1976.
4. Yorkston NJ, Zaki SA, Themen JFA, Havard CWH: Propranolol to control schizophrenic symptoms: 55 patients. Adv Clin Pharmacol 12:91–104, 1976.
5. May PRA: "Treatment of Schizophrenia." New York: Science House, Inc., 1968.
6. Davis JM: Dose equivalence of the antipsychotic drugs. J Psychiatr Res 11:65–69, 1974.
7. Overall JE, Gorham DR: The brief psychiatric rating scale. Psychol Rep 10:799–812, 1962.
8. Mellor CS: First rank symptoms of schizophrenia: I. The frequency in schizophrenics on admission to hospital. II. Differences between individual first rank symptoms. Br J Psychiatry 117:15–23, 1970.
9. Wing JK, Cooper JE, Sartorius N: "The Measurement and Classification of Psychiatric Symptoms." Cambridge: Cambridge University Press, 1974.
10. Masuoka D, Hansson E: Autoradiographic distribution studies of adrenergic blocking agents. II. ^{14}C-Propranolol, a beta-receptor-type blocker. Acta Pharmacol Toxicol 25:447–455, 1967.
11. Hayes A, Cooper RG: Studies on the absorption, distribution and excretion of propranolol in rat, dog and monkey, J Pharmacol Exp Ther 176:302–311, 1971.

12. Myers MG, Lewis PJ, Reid JL, Dollery CT: Brain concentration of propranolol in relation to hypotensive effect in the rabbit with observations on brain propranolol levels in man. J Pharmacol Exp Ther 192:327–335, 1975.
13. Gruzelier JH: Propranolol acts to modulate autonomic orienting and habituation processes in schizophrenia. This volume pp 99–118.
14. Pavlov IP: "Conditioned Reflexes and Psychiatry." New York: International Publisher's Co., 1941.
15. Pribram KH, McGuinness D: Arousal, activation, and effort in the control of attention. Psychol Rev 82:116–149, 1975.
16. Gruzelier JH, Venables PH: Skin conductance orienting activity in a heterogeneous sample of schizophrenics. J Nerv Ment Dis 155:277–287, 1972.
17. Gruzelier JH, Venables PH: Bimodality and lateral asymmetry of skin conductance orienting activity in schizophrenics: Replication and evidence of lateral asymmetry in patients with depression and disorders of personality. Biol Psychiatry 8:55–73, 1974.
18. Patterson T: Skin conductance responding/nonresponding and pupillometrics in chronic schizophrenia. J Nerv Ment Dis 163:200–209, 1976.
19. Gruzelier JH, Hammond NV: Schizophrenia: A dominant hemisphere temporal-limbic disorder? Res Commun Psychol Psychiatry Behav 1:33–72, 1976.
20. Gruzelier JH: Bimodal states of arousal and lateralized dysfunction in schizophrenia: The effect of chlorpromazine on psychophysiologic information processing and endocrine measures. In Wynne L, Cromwell R, Matthysse S (eds): "The Nature of Schizophrenia: New Findings and Future Strategies." New York: Wiley (in press).

3C. Some Practical Aspects of Using Propranolol in the Treatment of Schizophrenia

Neil J. Yorkston, Saniha Zaki, and C. W. H. Havard

INTRODUCTION

When large doses of propranolol were given every two to five hours to reduce the pulse and blood pressure in a patient psychotic from acute porphyria, the whole syndrome, including psychosis, remitted (1). Symptoms also remitted in patients with acute psychosis treated with propranolol every two to three hours in rapidly rising doses (increases of 400–600 mg/day) (2). Toxic reactions which were not already well known included ataxia and, rarely, a rise in blood pressure. The diagnosis of these patients was unclear from the published reports, but personal communication (3) makes it clear that at least some of these patients had a confusional state and that cases of chronic schizophrenia did not remit.

When this regimen was used with patients who had florid schizophrenic symptoms, the unusual toxic effects of propranolol were also encountered, and clinical improvement was at best only transient. The first three attempts were abandoned because of severe toxic effects, and a safer method of administration was developed (4). By using this safer regimen, florid schizophrenic symptoms sometimes remitted, and these remissions included individuals with long-standing illness. Relapse usually occurred within one to three days after stopping the drug.

Propranolol and Schizophrenia, pages 83–97

Before controlled studies were attempted, the first task was to ensure a safe system for giving propranolol. This paper outlines some practical points learned in treating a series of 55 patients with florid schizophrenic symptoms (5). It also draws on experience with toxic effects in other patients treated with propranolol but whose illnesses did not meet the criteria for this study.

PRACTICAL MANAGEMENT

The aim of treatment was to find the optimum dose of propranolol, alone or combined with a phenothiazine drug. Ideally, this dose would produce no toxic effects and symptoms would remit with restored insight.

At the risk of stating a truism, it was possible to give too little or too much. Too little was ineffective. Too much, particularly when the dose was raised too rapidly, resulted in toxic effects. The task then was to find the optimal dose for each individual patient. Signs of improvement, however slight, and even in the presence of gross psychotic behavior, were the best positive guide to the proper dose regimen. Signs of beta-blockade (lowered pulse rate and blood pressure) were taken as additional guidelines for the upper limits of dosage. The patients were watched carefully for early signs of toxicity, a warning that the dose was being increased too rapidly or had exceeded its safe upper limits.

To find and maintain the optimal dose, careful cooperation was required between the nursing and medical staffs in gaining the patients' collaboration. This involved continual reassessment of the patient between each dose of the drug, and particularly before each change in prescribed dosage.

It was important 1) to observe the patient carefully before treatment, 2) to look for early signs of improvement, 3) to monitor the pulse and blood pressure, 4) to watch for toxic signs and symptoms, 5) to keep accurate records, 6) to review progress continually, 7) to win the patient's sustained cooperation, and 8) maintain treatment.

1. Pretreatment Observation of the Patient

The observations of the whole staff were invaluable in managing the patient's treatment. Before treatment was started (for the reasons developed below), the staff observed the patient's general appearance, behavior, and coordination; the pinkness of his lips and ears; the style and content of his talk; as well as his pulse and blood pressure. Deviations from pretreatment norms alerted the staff to the presence of toxicity or to improvement.

A recurring difficulty was to convince patients, relatives, and staff of the need to continue the propranolol treatment after improvement occurred, particularly when the patients whose symptoms remitted felt and looked so well. A clear record of the original abnormal state was therefore a helpful reminder of how severely ill the patient was before treatment. The symptoms and signs of schizophrenia were recorded with the full psychiatric history, mental state, a questionnaire of the first rank symptoms of schizophrenia, and ratings on a modified (4) Brief Psychiatric Rating Scale (BPRS) (6, 7) and sometimes on the Present State Examination (8). A description of the patient's disturbed behavior was recorded so that relatives or the patient could be reminded of the obvious features of the illness, in case there was later a need to emphasize the importance of continuing treatment to prevent relapse.

2. Observation of Early Signs of Improvement

The most sensitive index of progress was the general clinical impression that the patient was improving. This was the best positive guide to dosage. Improvement was usually first apparent to the clinicians, but sometimes was more obvious either to the patient or to his relatives. The symptoms then gradually waned. Ratings on the BPRS often followed the clinical progress, giving a stricter, but delayed index of improvement.

In looking back, it seems likely that sometimes the dose was raised quickly through, and thus above, the therapeutic range, and that signs of early improvement were overlooked. Small signs of improvement served like straws in the wind, showing a change from a state of pathology to one of health. When a patient was improving, no matter how gross the obvious illness, it proved wise to persist with treatment at a constant or only gradually increasing dosage.

The earliest sign of improvement was a general impression that the patient looked better and seemed calmer. Most patients became less restless, irritable, or aggressive. They stopped staring into space or glancing furtively; their eyes no longer darted around, and they began to make normal social eye contacts. The general change was often apparent from the other side of the room. One patient dated improvement from his first dose; usually improvement was noticeable within a few days of starting propranolol. In three patients who did not appear noticeably calmer, plasma propranolol levels were found to be zero, which probably represented noncompliance.

Steady improvement in everyday behavior was often the best guide to progress. The order of improvement in other symptoms varied. The dimensions along which change was observed were variable, as the following examples suggest, and often direct questioning was required to establish that change was occurring.

As treatment progressed, coherent speech increased and disordered thought diminished. Patients who had been reserved or almost mute started to speak more freely. Previously secretive patients sometimes began to talk more about their delusions, hallucinations, or ideas of reference. This sometimes gave a misleading impression that they were deteriorating. However, subsequent improvement indicated that it was probably correct to regard the increased communication as a sign of improvement, even though the communication was of psychotic material. Warning may be taken from one patient who had, among a great deal of other disturbed behavior, disorganized suicidal thoughts and attempts. He committed suicide after he began to improve in insight and coherence. This emphasizes that a potentially suicidal patient may enter a more dangerous state when he begins to recover from schizophrenia, just as in the case of a potentially suicidal patient who is beginning to recover from severe depression. In both instances, the patient's thought and actions become more organized at a time when he is increasingly aware of his illness, but not yet convinced of his improvement.

Hallucinations usually faded slowly, but sometimes stopped abruptly. Sometimes, voices became quieter and quieter "like gradually turning down the hi-fi set." One patient said that spirits in his nose stopped speaking. During the next few weeks, the spirits progressively receded into the room, outside the window, away up in the sky, and finally disappeared. With others, the hallucinations came less frequently or occupied less time. Hallucinations stopped suddenly in five patients, who identified the day on which they stopped.

Ideas of reference diminished or stopped. However, the related delusional systems often seemed as strong as ever. The patients kept reiterating their false beliefs, but when asked for current supporting evidence, admitted that it was not continuing.

Delusions seemed to be the last symptom to remit. Sometimes, delusions stopped suddenly, for example, when hallucinations stopped suddenly. However, particularly in paranoid patients with delusions based on ideas of reference, delusions often took some weeks to remit after their active confirmation ceased.

Throughout the study, members of the staff were encouraged to keep affirming the ordinary facts of life, whenever appropriate, and to refrain from either agreeing with psychotic thought or offering speculative interpretations about it.

When the psychosis remitted, the patient usually felt well and looked well. Some patients could hardly believe the change. They usually became sociable and reasonable. Passers-by commented that they could not tell the difference between the patients in remission and the staff. The impression of normality was enhanced when several previously psychotic patients, who were familiar as isolated persons, were seen sitting in a group, neatly clothed, and conversing in a friendly, sensible way. Remission enhanced rehabilitation. A secretary who had been psychotic for most of 12 years and whose symptoms remitted one afternoon was able to type again when she first sat down at a typewriter.

Observers differed greatly in their ability to recognize the early beginnings of normal behavior, but this seemed to be a skill which was learned with practice. At first, some quite accurately commented that they had seen a given patient looking better before, referred to the obvious remaining psychotic features, and candidly could see no improvement. To effect remissions, it seemed essential to learn to notice continuing improvement as a guide to continuing a steady dosage.

3. Monitoring the Pulse and Blood Pressure

Pulse and blood pressure readings were usually taken with the patient sitting, two hours after taking propranolol. Lowered pulse and blood pressure readings were a useful guide to beta-blockade and thus to the dosage of propranolol. Another guide was to see if the pulse rate remained slow immediately after the patient stood up – the abolition of orthostatic tachycardia. The arbitrary physiological limit chosen was a pulse rate of 60/minute, although in some cases it was extended to 50/minute. When the pulse rate fell below the chosen rate, the total daily dose of propranolol was usually lowered by reducing both the twice-daily doses rather than omitting one of them. It was considered more important to give propranolol regularly twice a day than to be deterred by a slight drop in pulse or blood pressure. Propranolol was given twice daily because, at least with higher doses, it appeared to be effective for about 12 hours and because this proved to be a convenient regimen. It has certainly been demonstrated in hypertension that the hypotensive effect persists for 24 hours.

Similiarly, an arbitrary limit for blood pressure was chosen. This was usually 90/60 mm Hg, and rarely pressures of 85/50 mm Hg were accepted. If the blood pressure was below the chosen limit, the nursing staff contacted the psychiatrist who adjusted both the next dose and the prescription for the next day. Hypotension is not necessarily indicative of impaired perfusion and renal perfusion and hence urinary volume was always maintained. In a few cases, where a lower limit of systolic blood pressure was accepted, the blood urea was monitored at monthly intervals, and no significant changes were noted.

A rare toxic effect described by Steiner et al. (2) in eight patients who were given propranolol in large doses every few hours was a progressive and rapid rise in blood pressure. In our studies, this occurred only once when using ten doses per 24 hours to a total of 4.1 gm/day – a regimen we have now abandoned (4).

4. Watching for Toxic Symptoms and Signs

With hindsight, we sometimes found that patients who developed toxic signs had earlier experienced toxic symptoms. Reports of symptoms were therefore welcomed and carefully assessed. Severely psychotic patients sometimes described toxic symptoms quite clearly, although sometimes they described them in unusual terms. Symptoms we now regard as evidence of toxicity, until proved otherwise, are vivid visual hallucinations, and any kind of unsteadiness, dizziness, faintness, floating-on-air feeling, "seasickness," or poor balance. Abdominal discomfort, nausea, and vomiting disappeared when the drug was given after meals. Day and night staffs were asked to report any symptoms which the patients developed.

All staff members were encouraged to observe the patient's color, especially the pinkness of his lips and ears. Pallor was sometimes the first toxic sign. Lips and ears became remarkably pale; in one case, the pinnae were a pale yellow, cadaveric hue. Sometimes the nose, face, and lips also became pale. Pallor was noted within a few hours of raising the dosage of propranolol and disappeared after it was withheld for 4–24 hours. (Other causes of pallor needed to be considered, e.g., one patient who became very pale had a recurring hemorrhage from a hiatus hernia.) Dusky cyanosis was also seen occasionally. These circulatory changes occurred without further reductions in the pulse or blood pressure. Cold hands and feet are recognized side effects of beta-blockers in continual dosage, but the recognized circulatory changes were never startling in the dosage we were using.

Impaired coordination was another early sign of toxicity. The staff watched the patient's balance, observing the way he talked, walked, handled a knife or fork, and generally coordinated complex movements.

Slurred speech was sometimes the first sign of incoordination. In doubtful cases, observers could not always agree whether the speech had become slurred, as for example, if a patient spoke with an unfamiliar foreign or regional accent, or did not articulate clearly, or suffered from some dental or neurological defect. It was helpful, therefore, for the staff to be familiar with the patient's voice before propranolol was begun. Ideally, an audio-recording could give a basis for comparison.

A more unusual toxic sign was difficulty in coordinating movements of the upper limbs, such as clumsiness in writing or using cutlery. Difficulty with controlling the lower limbs was seen in unsteady walking, particularly when turning around, and difficulty in changing posture, as when the patient sat down or stood up. Sometimes, a patient flopped into a chair and was unable to get out of it. In the severest case, a patient fell when attempting to sit up in bed. Two fell out of bed. Some fell when walking. Three fell flat on their faces, apparently without using their hands to break the fall, and, respectively, sustained a black eye, a bleeding nose, and a cut lip. Transient neurological signs included nystagmus, past pointing, and dysdiadokokinesia.

The staff also noticed any change in the individual's pattern of abnormal behavior. Examples include a woman who became histrionically overactive, another who came uninvited into a ward round and crawled under a chair, and a third who lay on the floor kicking her legs while a ward round was in progress. All these new patterns of abnormal behavior, which were quite out of keeping with the individuals concerned, disappeared within a few hours of withholding propranolol, and so were presumably toxic effects. Another three patients became overactive and aggressive. Although these reactions at first were thought to be exacerbations of their illness, with hindsight it seems that they were probably toxic effects. The changes in abnormal behavior stopped when propranolol was withheld for a few hours and did not recur when lower doses were used.

Several patients who developed toxic effects at a given dose were able to tolerate that same dose later when it was introduced more gradually.

Other severe toxic effects included visual hallucinations and a confusional state. These severe toxic effects mainly occurred when propranolol was given frequently (four to ten doses per 24 hours) and when the daily dose was raised rapidly, for example, by 400–800 mg/day (3, 4). Severe toxic effects were uncommon in our later patients, presumably because propranolol was usually given only twice daily, the daily total dose was raised much more slowly (for example, by 40–80 mg/day), the individual doses were adjusted at the earliest signs of toxicity or of improvement, and the whole dosage schedules were changed more steadily.

5. Keep Accurate Records

Maintenance of careful records was essential. The nurses recorded every dose as given; and if a dose was missed, the reason was noted; for example, "slurred speech," "pulse 48," "refused," and "patient away." Graphing the dosage showed more vividly than a list whether the dosage schedule was irregular or steady.

Before the psychiatrist altered the prescription, he personally examined the patient with the above factors in mind and took into account several days' data from the pulse and blood pressure graphs and the record of the dose of propranolol given. He checked the dose that was given and not the prescribed dose. This was important because, for example, when an evening dose was omitted for any reason, the total for the day would be only half the quantity prescribed. All prescriptions were made with the proviso that propranolol would be withheld if there were toxic symptoms or if there was unresolved doubt about the pulse or blood pressure.

6. Continued Review of Patient's Progress

Safe treatment required the patient to be reviewed continually. The prescriber examined the patient on every day on which the dose was being increased. Conversely, on days when the patient was not personally assessed, the drug was not increased. When a steady dose was reached, it was still wise for the psychiatrist to review the patient two or three times a week because early toxicity sometimes occurred after a dose had been continued for several days or because a further increment was indicated.

7. Win the Patient's Cooperation

Sustained, tactful persuasion was needed to help some patients to take their tablets regularly. It was explained to patients who improved or remitted that propranolol was essential for their recovery. The staff stressed that improvement followed taking the tablets regularly. Patients were also frequently asked about the importance of their tablets, and their statements about the value of the tablets were confirmed. In the case of individuals who stopped the tablets and relapsed, this sequence was spelled out to them, and the example was quoted to others. Early relapse was accompanied by insight for up to 12 to 24 hours. Two patients who asked for help within this time responded to a modest increase in the dose. Within days of starting relapse, patients usually lost insight again, did not seek help, and usually proved more difficult to treat at the next attempt. Patients were therefore warned, should relapse occur, to seek help at once.

8. Maintain Treatment

The main danger was from stopping treatment. Those who stopped propranolol almost invariably relapsed. Because relapses were so severe and so hard to treat again, we recommend continuing propranolol, often at a high dose and at least in small doses, for example, 40–80 mg twice daily.

DOSAGE

Propranolol tablets are bitter and when chewed were a source of complaint or even delusional misinterpretation. The patients were therefore encouraged to swallow whole tablets quickly.

One patient complained of unpleasant sensations which might relate to the local anesthetic action of propranolol.

We learned that every dose counted. A regular dosage was needed to bring about an even response. A regular dosage schedule allowed the level to be adjusted steadily, avoiding toxicity from a sudden increase in dosage or relapse through missing doses.

After a test dose of 10 or 20 mg of propranolol, the patient's general condition, pulse, and blood pressure were observed for two hours in case of the rare event of malaise, bronchospasm, or cardiovascular collapse. Not one patient in this series of studies had untoward effects, although some with neuroses took an immediate, intense dislike to the drug. The first full dose was 40 mg followed by 40 or 80 mg four to eight hours later. The next day, 80 mg was given twice daily.

The psychiatrist assessed the patient before prescribing each increment in dose. The same dose was maintained if the patient was improving or had reached the planned limits of pulse and blood pressure. The daily total was reduced if the pulse or blood fell below the desired limits. If toxic symptoms or signs developed, the next dose was postponed, reduced, or omitted; the total daily dose was lowered and divided equally between the morning and evening doses. The dosage schedules have not been analyzed, but the present rate at which we raise the dose for patients with schizophrenia (for example, by 40–80 mg/day) is about one-tenth of Atsmon's rate of increase (by 400–800 mg/day) for patients with acute psychosis.

Regular dosage, twice every day, with steady, gradual increases from day to day, appeared the ideal way to stabilize a patient. In contrast, patients who kept missing doses seemed to take longer to stabilize and were more likely to develop toxic symptoms. Therefore, if a patient missed the evening dose, the night staff ensured that it was given later to maintain regular treatment.

Propranolol was given after meals (and any extra doses were also given with food), as some patients who took it on an empty stomach complained of nausea or abdominal discomfort. Alimentary symptoms rarely made it necessary to reduce the dose.

Treatment of Toxic Effects

With the above regimen, toxic effects became uncommon. The first three attempts were stopped because of toxic effects (4), but no further course of treatment was broken off because of toxic effects (5). Thirty-two patients were free from toxic effects. In practice, no specific treatment of toxic effects was necessary in our series, since even the severe effects subsided within hours when propranolol was withheld. Cardiac failure in one patient responded to the standard treatment. Specialist medical cover and a supply of emergency drugs were always available, however. Isoprenaline is a beta-receptor agonist and hence the natural antidote to excessive beta-adrenergic blockade. However, it requires intravenous administration and may produce cardiac arrhythmias. Safer alternatives are available and are usually adequate. If isoprenaline is given, it should be administered in an intravenous drip with 2 mg of isoprenaline in 500 ml of 5% dextrose. The initial rate of infusion should be 5 drops/minute, and this can be increased according to the clinical indications.

Aminophylline is the most useful drug for bronchospasm precipitated by beta-blockers. It should be given in a dose of 250–500 mg by slow, intravenous administration. It is much safer than isoprenaline.

Atropine (0.5 mg intravenously or intramuscularly) is useful to combat the unopposed vagal activity association with beta-adrenergic blockade. It is therefore useful if bradycardia is severe.

Hypotension rarely requires treatment as it is unusual for propranolol to produce a severe degree of hypotension. Even with systolic pressure of 80 mm Hg, perfusion is usually adequate; and if symptoms of dizziness or faintness are present, the patient should lie down. Atropine should be given if bradycardia is severe.

In the rare event of hypertension complicating propranolol administration, phentolamine (5 mg) given intravenously is the quickest method of correcting the hypertension and is indicated in an emergency situation. More commonly, the hypertension does not require emergency measures and can be controlled by oral phenoxybenzamine in an initial dose of 10 mg every eight hours.

Hypoglycemia may be precipitated by large doses of propranolol, but it is readily controlled by oral doses of glucose.

Cardiac failure precipitated by propranolol should be treated in the standard way with digoxin and diuretics, and the dose of propranolol should be reduced slowly and eventually withdrawn. Propranolol should not be discontinued suddenly as there is a risk of precipitating severe angina in patients with ischaemic heart disease.

Drug Combinations

Propranolol was substituted for, or added to, the patient's regime of medical treatment. If possible, propranolol was given alone; but if the schizophrenic symptoms did not remit, a phenothiazine drug, usually trifluoroperazine, was added. Sometimes propranolol was added to an existing drug regimen.

Some patients whose symptoms remitted while taking both propranolol and a phenothiazine drug became tired, drowsy, or "depressed" (but did not develop an affective disorder). A man who complained of lethargy, a symptom which might easily be attributed to propranolol, regained his energy and concentration when trifluoroperazine was stopped. Another remained drowsy for nearly 24 hours after a single, inadvertant dose of 50 mg of chlorpromazine. Two patients on high doses of propranolol repeatedly became unduly aggressive after drinking alcohol, but this association was not constant.

Maintenance or Relapse

When the schizophrenic symptoms remitted, the patients felt and looked well. They were lucid, alert, and lacked the apathetic, unreactive appearance of many patients who are stabilized on phenothiazine drugs. "Schizophrenia" scores on the BPRS had fallen to zero. Remissions usually seemed sustained, at least in the short term, as long as propranolol was maintained. The length of follow-up of remissions varied from ten days to 20 months.

Two patients whose symptoms remitted, and who later stopped propranolol, had insight into early relapse and immediately returned for advice. Their symptoms were controlled again by increasing the dose of propranolol. Patients whose symptoms relapsed for longer than one to three days usually quickly lost insight, and it seemed more difficult to stabilize them again. When one patient, who had remitted, stopped taking the drug, the symptoms returned with loss of insight; but when propranolol was started again, the symtoms remitted again. He repeated the cycle five times. One patient whose symptoms remitted for about ten days has not been stabilized again in spite of repeated attempts for over 12 months.

CONCLUSION

The present treatment regime appears almost to have eliminated the severe toxic reactions that occurred when propranolol was given every few hours (four to ten times per 24 hours), and the daily dose was raised rapidly by 400–800 mg/day. At present, we think that giving two doses per day and raising the daily total by about one-tenth of that rate is nearer to the optimal method. Although the pulse and blood pressure readings are valuable, the best guide to dosage remains the examination of the patient's mental state.

ACKNOWLEDGMENTS

We thank the nursing staff at Friern Hospital for their careful observations, Dr. H. A. Johnston for his advice, ICI Pharmaceuticals Division for a research grant, Mrs. Michele Johnstone for her secretarial help, Mrs. E. Ames, Medical Librarian, Friern Hospital and editors of the Postgraduate Medical Journal for permission to publish this expanded version of an earlier paper.

REFERENCES

1. Atsmon A, Blum I, Fischl J: Treatment of an acute attack of porphyria variegata with propranolol. S Afr Med J 46:311–314, 1972.
2. Steiner M, Blum I, Wijsenbeek H, Atsmon A: Results of the treatment of psychoses with propranolol. Kupat Holim Yearbook 2:201–209, 1972.
3. Atsmon A: Personal communication, 1975.
4. Yorkston NJ, Zaki SA, Malik MKU, Morrison RC, Havard CWH: Propranolol in the control of schizophrenic symptoms. Br Med J 4:633–635, 1974.
5. Yorkston NJ, Zaki SA, Themen JFA, Havard CWH: Propranolol to control schizophrenic symptoms: 55 patients. Adv Clin Pharmacol 12:91–104, 1976.
6. Overall JE, Gorham DR: The brief psychiatric rating scale. Psychol Rep 10:799, 1962.
7. Turner WJ: "Glossaries for Use with the Overall and Gorham Brief Psychiatric Rating Scale and for a Modified Malamud-Sands Rating Scale." Research Division, Central Islip State Hospital, Central Islip, New York, 1963.
8. Wing JK, Cooper JE, Sartorius N: "The Measurement and Classification of Psychiatric Symptoms." Cambridge: Cambridge University Press, 1974.

3D. Propranolol Acts to Modulate Autonomic Orienting and Habitutation Processes in Schizophrenia

John H. Gruzelier

INTRODUCTION

Similarities have been drawn between the behavioral effects of propranolol and the behavioral functions of the amygdala (22). The amygdala together with the hippocampus exert a modulatory control over the hypothalamus and thereby affect the regulation of the visceroautonomic system, emotional expression, and learning and conditioning processes (23). An example of this modulatory control is reflected in the autonomic orienting response and its rate of habituation. Orderly behavior, whether it involves an emotional or intellectual response, requires the focusing upon (*orienting* towards) an appropriate stimulus and disregarding it (*habituating* to it) when the significance of the stimulus has been appraised. This can be demonstrated in the laboratory by observing the electrodermal response, often termed the GSR, to a pure tone of moderate intensity, and watching it diminish with each successive tone presentation. Amygdalectomized monkeys do not show these processes of first orienting to the sound, and then habituating to it. They show one of two patterns – either they fail to exhibit responses at all, or their responses fail to extinguish as the sound is repeated. Hippocampal monkeys show deficits of habituation (10–12, 24).

Schizophrenics display electrodermal orienting patterns similar to those of amygdalectomized monkeys. Approxi-

Propranolol and Schizophrenia, pages 99–118

mately 50% of schizophrenics at virtually all stages of the disorder show a deficit of habituation to meaningless sounds. Another 50% exhibit few or no responses at all (7, 8, 12). Evidence from many sources points to the involvement of temporal-limbic processes in schizophrenia. It is conceivable that the efficacy of propranolol in schizophrenia (3, 25, 26) results through the restoring of temporal-limbic functions, such as those of the amygdala and hippocampus. This hypothesis was tested by examining the electrodermal orienting responses of untreated schizophrenics and those treated with propranolol, phenothiazines, and propranolol + phenothiazines, and comparing the results with those obtained in a suitable control population. It was shown previously that chlorpromazine, the best known phenothiazine, does not have systematic effects upon the electrodermal orienting response, though it does produce a reduction in levels of sweat gland activity (10). If propranolol facilitates the temporal-limbic functions attributable, at least in part, to the amygdalae, then it should both increase the rate of habituation in patients who show a lack of it and restore orienting responses in those patients who fail to exhibit them. The results to be reported here are consistent with the above hypothesis.

SUBJECTS AND DRUG TREATMENT GROUPS

The schizophrenic patients were divided on the basis of drug treatment into three equal groups of 36 patients. One group did not receive drugs, another was on phenothiazines, and the third was treated with propranolol, either alone (17 cases) or in combination with phenothiazines (19 cases). Some patients were included more than once but under different treatment conditions. Fourteen were tested without drugs as well as on phenothiazines, 11 on phenothiazines and later on propranolol, and 8 were tested without drugs and then on propranolol. Pertinent information about the patients studied is shown in Table I.

All patients were diagnosed as being unambiguously schziophrenic by the psychiatric team. The patients on propranolol participated either in the open study of 55 cases (see pp 39–67,

TABLE I. Description of Patient Population*

Variables		Groups: propranolol	no drugs	phenothiazines
Sex				
Male		22	26	31
Female		14	10	5
Age (yrs)	$\bar{x}$	35	38	39
	range	18–59	18–57	22–52
Age at first	$\bar{x}$	25	27	25
onset (yr)	range	16–56	15–50	16–45
Number of	$\bar{x}$	5	3	5
admissions	range	1–13	1–13	1–24
Total time	$\bar{x}$	7 yr 23 wk	8 yr 20 wk	11 yr 5 wk
in hospital	range	4 wk–30 yr	1 wk–30 yr	3 wk–26 yr

*Sex, age, age of first onset of hospital admissions and total length of time in hospital.

this volume) or were in two controlled studies in which propranolol was either added to existing phenothiazine medication (see pp 69–82, this volume) or was compared with chlorpromazine in patients newly admitted to the hospital and under the direction of Dr. N. Yorkston and Professor S. Hirsch (unpublished). Fourteen of the patients were included in controlled studies, in which cases the experimenters did not know what medication the patients were receiving. The patients on phenothiazines were treated by several other consultant psychiatrists at Friern and Charing Cross Hospitals.

The untreated group consisted either of patients newly admitted to the hospital and free of drugs having long-term effects, or of chronic hospitalized patients who had been withdrawn from such drugs for more than four weeks. Members of the untreated group, as a whole, had fewer hospital admissions than those on propranolol ($t = 2.90$, $df = 1.70$, $p < 0.001$) or phenothiazines ($t = 2.24$, $df = 1.70$, $p < 0.025$). However, their total times in the hospital were similar, and there were no other differences between the variables in Table I. Doses of propranolol and phenothiazines are shown in Table II.

TABLE II. Treatment Groups and Doses

Group	Means and ranges of doses (mg/day)	
Propranolol alone	Propranolol	605 (160–1,920)
Propranolol combined with	Propranolol	420 (160–1,500)
phenothiazines	Phenothiazines	355 (50–1,071)
Phenothiazines	Phenothiazines	779 (74–2,976)

In addition, 36 normal nonpatient volunteers were tested. Their mean age was 32 years, ranging from 29 to 47. They were younger than the patients ($0.05 > p > 0.01$). Correlations between skin conductance variables and age were insignificant, and therefore, the small differences in age between the groups did not affect the results.

When patients were tested more than once, at least eight weeks elapsed before retesting. Psychiatrists in charge of treatment referred patients for testing when there was a continuing favorable response to treatment. Close to the date of testing, the Brief Psychiatric Rating Scale, as modified by Yorkston et al (3) was administered by Drs. Zaki and Yorkston. Patients on both propranolol and phenothiazines improved.

PROCEDURES

Skin conductance orienting responses were examined to 1,000 Hz tones (70 dB, one second) presented 13 times at intervals varying between 20 and 40 seconds. Skin conductance was measured bilaterally from bipolar placements on the distal phalanges of the first and second fingers of each hand. Silver-silver chloride electrodes were attached with Beckman electrolyte and connected to a direct current skin conductance measurement device modified from the design of Lykken and Venables (4). This dual-channel system was connected to preamplifiers of either a Grass model 7D polygraph in the Charing Cross laboratory or to a San Ei rectigraph in the Friern laboratory. The orienting stimuli were recorded on cassette and presented from a Sony recorder type TE – 153 SD through Koss type 6LC headphones at Charing Cross and Sansui type 55-2 headphones at Friern.

In the Friern laboratory the subject sat alone in a sound-attenuated room. At Charing Cross, the subject was in the same room as the experimenter at a distance of 1.5 m and facing away from the recording apparatus. Recording began approximately two minutes after instructing the subject. While the electrodes were fastened in place, the purpose of the recording session was explained to the subject as a routine procedure that would assist the doctors in deciding appropriate treatment. The recordings were explained to be a measure of the subject's state of relaxation. In passing, it was mentioned that headphones would be placed on the subject to screen out noises in the laboratory and that there would be occasional sounds through the headphones which would assist in determining state of relaxation. The subjects were asked to find a comfortable sitting position and asked not to move during the recording session. Movements, coughs, vocalizations, etc., were noted on the chart and these sections of the trace were deleted during scoring.

An orienting response was operationally defined as occurring between 0.8 and 5.0 seconds after stimulus onset. Responses outside this interval were considered as spontaneous fluctuations. A minimum criterion of 1 mm was adopted. The maximum gain setting was 0.05 μmho/cm. The scoring was carried out blindly by trained assistants.

RESULTS

Distribution of Orienting Responses

In the nonpatient control group (Fig. 1) the distribution of orienting responses was normal. All but two subjects exhibited responses which diminished as the tone was repeated. However, the number of trials to reach a conventional habituation criterion of three successive "no response" followed a bimodal distribution. At one extreme of the distribution were found the majority of subjects (28), whose responses habitu-

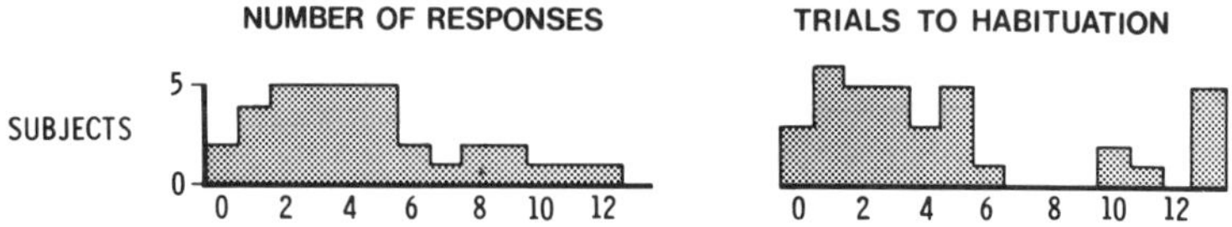

Fig. 1. Normal controls. Number of subjects on the ordinate and trials on the abscissa.

ated normally. The scores of this subgroup approximated a normal distribution. At the other extreme were three subjects who were slow in habituating and five who failed to habituate. Thus, while the majority of nonpatient volunteers habituated normally, a small subgroup tended to overreact to the orienting sounds.

The orienting responses and trials to habituation of untreated schizophrenic patients both followed a bimodal distribution (Fig. 2). However, the bimodality was of a different form from that found in the trials to habituation of the control group. More than half of the patients were found at one extreme of the distribution. These patients all exhibited no arousal reactions. The other extreme consisted largely of patients whose responses were slow in habituating. Similar results had been found in institutionalized schizophrenic patients withdrawn from drug treatment (5, 6).

Phenothiazine drugs did not correct the failure to orient or the slowness in habituating (Fig. 3). The distributions of responses and trials to habituation of untreated patients and those on phenothiazines were similar. Differences between the latter two groups with Fisher's Exact Probability Test were not significant, while all comparisons of these groups with the control group were highly significant ($p < 0.001$).

The bimodality found with patients on phenothiazines replicated earlier results both of the author and colleagues (5, 7–10) and of others (11–13).

The responses of patients treated with propranolol are shown in Fig. 4. Nonresponders were reduced to approximately half the number found with untreated schizophrenic patients or those on phenothiazines, and nonhabituators were absent altogether. All patients exhibited less than six responses

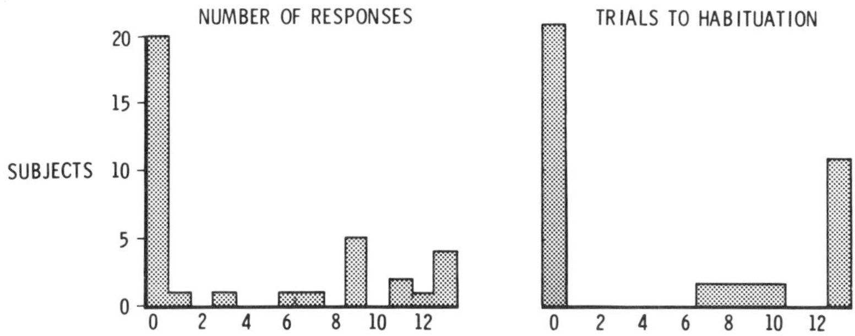

Fig. 2. Schizophrenic patients not on drugs.

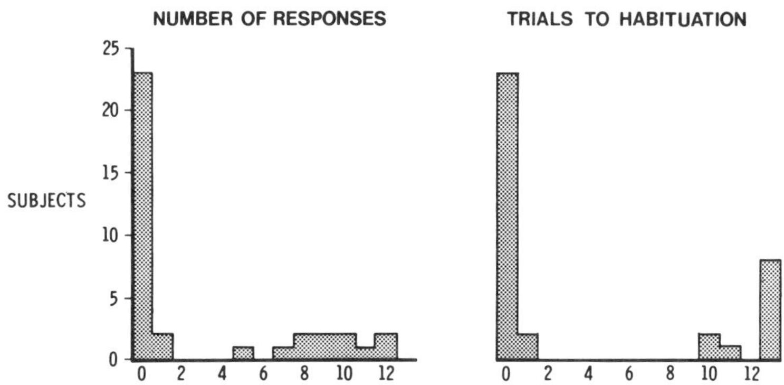

Fig. 3. Schizophrenic patients on phenothiazines.

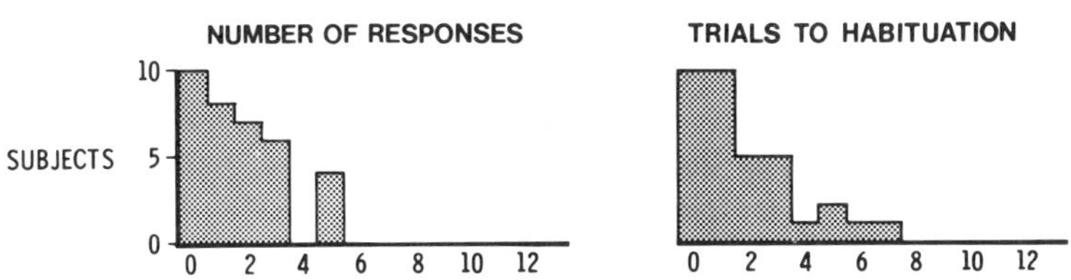

Fig. 4. Schizophrenic patients on propranolol.

and all habituated by trial 7. In both respects there was no difference between patients on propranolol alone and those on propranolol combined with phenothiazines. Comparisons between propranolol-treated patients and patients on phenothiazines or not on drugs were all highly significant (see Table III).

TABLE III. Comparisons of Numbers of Responses and Trials to Habituation*

Groups	No. of responses	Trials to habituation
Propranolol (P) and propranolol (P) + phenothiazines (PT)	ns	ns
P and PT	$p < 0.001$	$p < 0.001$
P and no drug (ND)	$p < 0.001$	$p < 0.001$
P and control (C)	$p < 0.001$	$p < 0.04$
PT and ND	ns	ns
PT and C	$p < 0.001$	$p < 0.001$
ND and C	$p < 0.001$	$p < 0.001$

*Probability levels from comparisons with Fisher's Exact Probability Test with subjects catagorized as having 0, 1–6 or 7–13 responses or trials to habituation.

Patients on propranolol alone also differed from normal volunteers. Response habituation was faster in the patients than in the controls ($p = 0.002$). This strengthening of habituation was the clearest effect of the drug. After showing clinical improvement, not one of the patients on propranolol continued to overreact to the novel sounds. While there were fewer nonresponders on propranolol (10 cases) than there were on phenothiazines (23 cases) or among those not on drugs (20 cases), still no response occurred in greater numbers in the propranolol-treated patients than among the normal volunteers. The subgroup that failed to orient despite propranolol tended clinically to be the most resistant to treatment.

The finding of fewer schizophrenic nonresponders in the propranolol group than in other treatment groups indicates that the drug did not simply lower responsivity by increasing habituation. It seemed to produce a modulation of orienting activity, reducing responses in nonhabituators and reinstating responses in nonresponders.

Amplitude of the Orienting Reaction

The amplitude of the orienting reflex is thought to reflect both the strength of the arousal reaction and the level of tonic excitation in the response system (14). In normal subjects, habituation usually follows an exponential course, beginning with a rapid, negatively accelerated decline in amplitude until responses cease altogether. In some cases, the process of habituation is less regular. The reaction may grow in strength for two or three trials before a habituation decrement begins. Sometimes habituation is not sustained for long, and reorienting occurs. In the latter case, the arousal reaction usually then diminishes with repetition, but occasionally may increase progessively.

We have examined: 1) the strength of the arousal reaction regardless of whether it began on early or late trials; 2) the rate at which the arousal reaction habituated; 3) the level of responding at the time when responses reached plateau (thought to reflect tonic reactivity in the response system); and 4) the extent of differences in the reaction between the right and left hands.

Two effects have been found consistently in all previous studies. The rate at which the arousal reaction habituates before reaching an asymptote appears to depend on the amplitude of the reaction; the higher the amplitude the faster the rate of habituation (15). This was also the case in the present study. Propranolol had powerful effects on response habituation, all patients habituating by trial 7, while even in the control group some subjects continued responding. Response amplitudes on late trials, as distinct from early ones, were significantly lower in the patients on propranolol than in subjects in all other groups. Propranolol, therefore, had the effect of reducing the level of tonic activity in the response system.

In the control group, the overall form of response habituation was normal (Fig. 5). In the group as a whole, response amplitudes were highest on the first trial and reached an asymptote on the fifth trial, by which time most subjects had stopped responding. The rates of responding and habituation were similar for both hands.

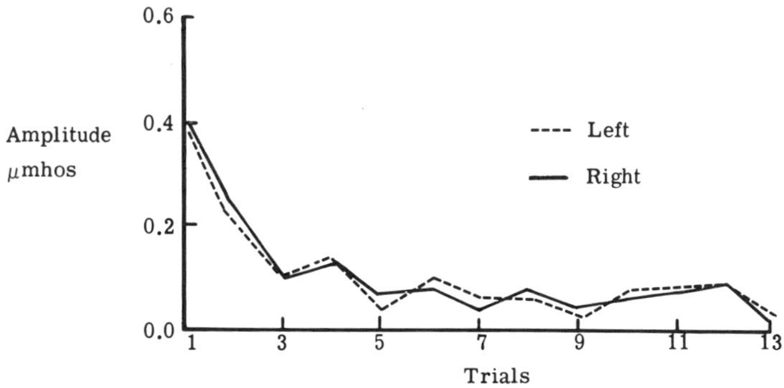

Fig. 5. Bilateral orienting response amplitudes of the controls.

Response habituations in untreated schizophrenic patients, those on phenothiazines, and those on propranolol alone or combined with phenothiazines are shown in Figs. 6–9. The untreated patients differed from the controls in having stronger reactions ($F = 5.05$, $df = 1.49$, $p = 0.029$) and in showing more reactivity in their response systems ($F = 19.61$, $df = 1.49$, $p < 0.001$). The course of habituation in these patients was less regular and was bilaterally asymmetrical (Fig. 6).

The pattern of habituation of patients on phenothiazines resembled that of the untreated group. The arousal reactions were stronger than those of the control group ($F = 8.00$, $df = 1.45$, $p = 0.007$) and there was more tonic activity in the response systems ($F = 6.71$, $df = 1.45$, $p < 0.001$). Furthermore, habituation of the arousal reaction tended to occur more quickly on the right than the left hand in patients, while the controls showed no bilateral differences ($F = 3.12$, $df = 1.45$, $p = 0.08$). Bilateral asymmetry in the same direction was found in the measure of tonic activity in the response system ($F = 5.81$, $df = 1.45$, $p = 0.02$). On all these measures the untreated and phenothiazine-treated groups did not differ from each other (Figs. 6, 7).

The stronger reactions in those schizophrenic patients who exhibit responses when compared with normal controls replicates earlier results both with phenothiazine-treated patients (7–9) and others not receiving drugs (5). This was true of the magnitude of the initial arousal reactions, the irregularities of

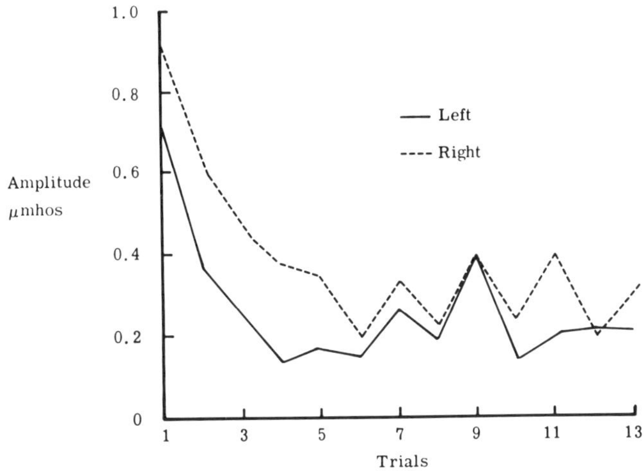

Fig. 6. Bilateral orienting response amplitudes of patients not on drugs.

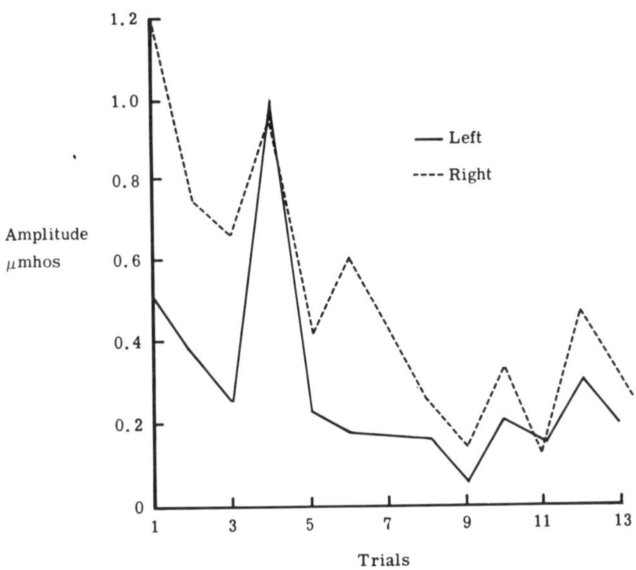

Fig. 7. Bilateral orienting response amplitudes of patients on phenothiazines.

habituation, and the levels of tonic activity in the response systems. The evidence of bilateral asymmetries in the direction of larger responses on the right than the left hand in patients also replicates earlier results in treated and untreated patients

(5, 6, 8, 9, 16). Here this was true of the initial arousal reaction as well as of the tonic responses on later trials. The faster habituation of the arousal reaction on the right than the left hand in patients is consistent with the evidence that habituation of responses on early trials is a function of the amplitude of the response.

Response habituation on propranolol resembled habituation in normal volunteers more closely than that of schizophrenic patients on other treatments. This was especially apparent in those receiving the combined treatment of phenothiazines and propranolol (Fig. 8). In the latter group, resemblance to the normal volunteers was found in the magnitude of the arousal reaction as well as in its bilateral symmetry.

An interaction between propranolol and phenothiazines was most apparent in the strength of the arousal reaction. Reactions in groups on either drug alone were similar in magnitude. The addition of propranolol to phenothiazines reduced response amplitudes, as indicated by the lower response amplitudes of patients on the combined medication when compared with those on propranolol alone ($F = 5.58$, $df = 1.26$, $p = 0.03$) (compare Fig. 8 with Fig. 9). Patients receiving only propranolol or phenothiazines only showed higher response amplitudes than did the control group ($F = 5.30$, $df = 1.47$, $p = 0.03$).

Patients on propranolol alone had higher right- than left-hand response amplitudes when compared with normal volunteers ($F = 4.19$, $df = 1.7$, $p = 0.05$), as did patients on phenothiazines alone ($F = 5.30$, $df = 1.24$, $p = 0.02$). However, when phenothiazines were combined with propranolol there was no bilateral asymmetry ($F = 0.05$, $df = 1.11$, ns).

To summarize, responding schizophrenic patients exhibited orienting reflexes that tended to be stronger than those found in normal individuals. The same was true of the level of tonic excitability in the response system. Habituation of responses tended to occur at a faster rate. It appeared to be weaker in patients than in normal controls, since in some instances habituation failed to be sustained and reorienting occurred, often

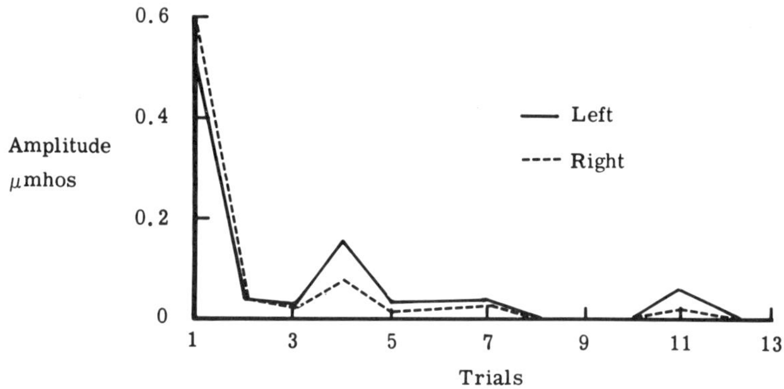

Fig. 8. Bilateral orienting response amplitudes of patients on propranolol combined with phenothiazines.

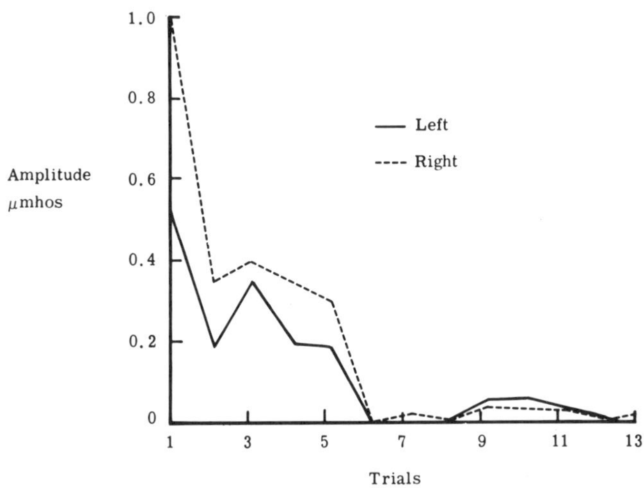

Fig. 9. Bilateral orienting response amplitudes of patients on propranolol alone.

with the strength of the arousal reaction increasing progressively in magnitude. However, more than half of the schizophrenic patients failed to show any arousal reactions at all.

As indicated in the previous section, the most pronounced effect of propranolol on the orienting reaction was to strengthen the process of habituation to repetition of the orienting stimulus. Consistent with the dual-process theory of habituation (14), the increase in habituation coincided with a lower level of tonic excitability in the response system than was found even in many normal volunteers. The action of the drug could not be simply a reduction in the strength of the arousal reaction because of decreased activity in the reflex pathways, since there were fewer schizophrenic patients without orienting responses among those treated with propranolol. This suggested that in some patients activity in the orienting reflex system was being increased by propranolol.

From a psychophysiological point of view, reactions in patients on propranolol were more appropriate to the context. They occurred on the first trial when the stimulus was novel, and then, since the stimulus had no meaning to the patient, progressively and smoothly subsided without showing the irregularities of habituation found in the responses of many patients on other treatments and in some controls. Propranolol appeared to regulate the emission of responses, possibly through strengthening a central gating mechanism. Administered together, propranolol and the phenothiazines reduced the strength of the arousal reaction to normal levels and minimized bilateral asymmetries in responses. Both features were abnormal in patients on either propranolol alone or phenothiazines alone, as well as in untreated patients. This effect may reflect reduced activity in the orienting reflex pathways which occurs only when the drugs are combined.

Resting Skin Conductance Levels

With the exception of those on propranolol and phenothiazines combined, schizophrenic patients had higher levels of resting skin conductance than the controls (Fig. 10). As with the orienting reaction, the combined treatment appeared to return electrodermal activity to within normal limits.

Propranolol appeared possibly to increase levels of sweating since patients receiving propranolol alone had slightly higher levels of skin conductance than those on the combined treatment ($F = 3.41$, $df = 1.34$, $p = 0.07$). This was not the case in patients on phenothiazines alone or in untreated patients. Therefore, the effects of propranolol in restoring habituation of the orienting reflex cannot be attributed to a blocking of the peripheral sweat mechanism.

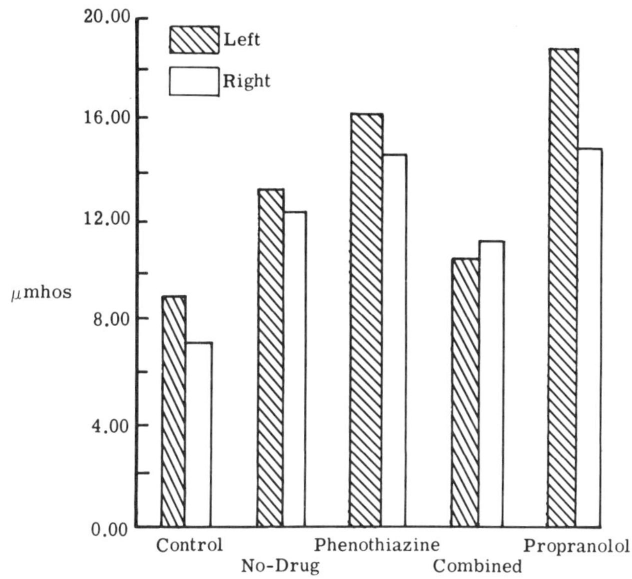

Fig. 10. Resting bilateral skin conductance levels.

Earlier it was found that among schizophrenic patients group differences were found in levels of skin conductance and other autonomic measures, as well as in plasma cortisol and information processing capacities that vary with changes in cortical arousal (17). Levels of arousal were higher in patients with orienting responses than in those without them. Correlations between level of arousal and such diverse measures as mentioned above rarely have been found in normal subjects (18). The more aroused group of patients also tended to have higher right- than left-hand levels of skin conductance, while the converse was true of the less aroused group (8, 9, 19). Right-hand directionality occurs when the organism is activated, while left-hand directionality correlates with states of relaxation or low arousal.

The presence or absence of orienting responses did not coincide with different states of arousal in propranolol-treated individuals; skin conductance levels of responders and nonresponders did not differ. Schizophrenic patients on propranolol alone were like normal controls in having bilateral differences in skin conductance levels in the direction of higher levels on the left than the right hand (propranolol, $F = 12.62$, $df = 1.16$, $p = 0.003$; controls, $F = 13.03$, $df = 1.35$, $p < 0.001$) after subjects had become adapted to laboratory conditions. The magnitude of the effect was larger in the patients on propranolol ($\bar{x}$ 3.9 μmho) than in the normal controls ($\bar{x}$ 1.8 μmho); ($F = 4.09$, $df = 1.51$, $p = 0.05$) (Fig. 10). Although propranolol tended to increase levels of sweating, this effect appeared to be counteracted by phenothiazines when the two drugs are given in combination (Fig. 10).

Spontaneous Fluctuations in Skin Conductance

Spontaneous fluctuations in skin conductance often are regarded as an index of central arousal. The rate of fluctuations varies not so much with cognitive arousal as with emotional arousal, viz., when an individual is under the threat of receiving shock (19, 20). Since schizophrenia, by definition, is a condition in which the individual appears to be particularly vulnerable to threat, spontaneous fluctuations are of special relevance.

Phenothiazines have been shown to reduce both the number and time course of spontaneous electrodermal fluctuations in chronic schizophrenic patients (6). This may be attributable partially to the peripheral cholinergic blocking properties of phenothiazines. Phenothiazine-treated patients in the current study showed fewer spontaneous fluctuations than either the control group ($F = 7.00$, $df = 1.70$, $p < 0.001$) or the untreated patients ($F = 3.75$, $df = 1.70$, $p < 0.005$) (see Fig. 11). The patients receiving both propranolol and phenothiazines showed values between those of the control group and those of the patients on phenothiazines alone. Patients treated with propranolol showed such a wide variance that the means for this group were not significantly different from those of any of the other groups examined.

In replication of earlier studies, significant differences were found between patients with and without orienting responses both when off drugs or when on phenothiazines. Responders had more spontaneous fluctuations than nonresponders in both the untreated ($F = 6.14$, $df = 1.34$, $p = 0.02$) and the phenothiazine-treated ($F = 3.96$, $df = 1.34$, $p = 0.05$) groups.

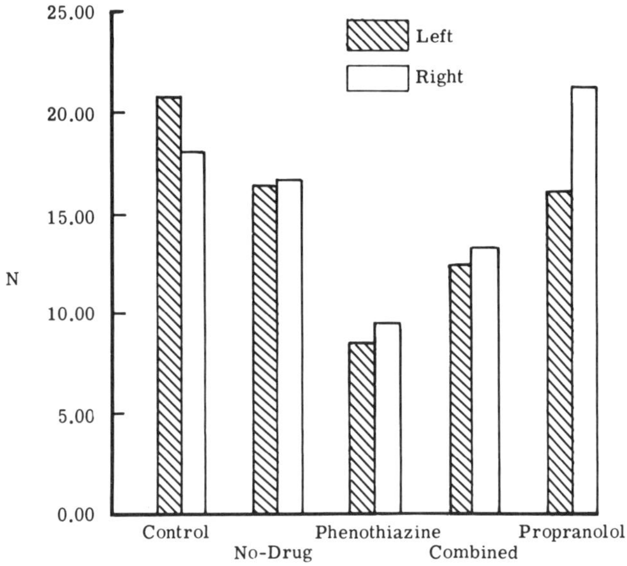

Fig. 11. Bilateral incidence of spontaneous fluctuations in skin conductance in individuals at rest.

As in the case of skin conductance levels, bilateral differences in opposite directions in responders and nonresponders were found in the spontaneous fluctuations of the untreated patients (F = 4.44, df = 1.34, p = 0.04). The means for the patients on phenothiazines varied in the same direction but were not significantly different (p = 0.12). Instead, there was a tendency for the group as a whole to have a higher incidence of spontaneous fluctuations on the right than on the left hand (F = 3.89, df = 1.35, p = 0.05). The opposite asymmetry was found in the control group (F = 5.35, df = 1.35, p = 0.025) (Fig. 11).

In patients on propranolol, as with the normal controls, there was no significant association between orienting responses and spontaneous fluctuations. However, none of the schizophrenic patient groups, regardless of drug treatment, exhibited the left-hand directionality of spontaneous fluctuations found in the control group. Comparisons of bilateral differences between the control group and all of the schizophrenic groups were significant at levels ranging from $p < 0.01$ to $p < 0.004$.

The absence of any differences in the rate of spontaneous fluctuations between patients on propranolol and patients on phenothiazine or on no drug treatment, as well as normal volunteers, indicates the highly specific nature of modulation of the skin conductance orienting reaction by propranolol that was discussed above.

SUMMARY

Propranolol, in contrast to phenothiazines or no drug treatment, had the following effects on autonomic arousal reactions and their rate of habituation in schizophrenic patients.

1) Those patients on propranolol who had electrodermal responses showed faster habituation of the responses than did patients on other treatments or many normal volunteers.

2) There were 50% fewer patients without orienting reactions in the group treated with propranolol than in the groups receiving other treatments.

3) Differences in extent of the arousal reaction and the bilateral asymmetry found in the schizophrenic patients were unaffected by propranolol treatment.

4) Levels of sweating were slightly higher in patients on propranolol, suggesting that the facilitation of habituation was not attributable to a peripheral depressant effect of the drug.

5) Spontaneous fluctuations in skin conductance, which are reduced by phenothiazines, were unaffected by propranolol. This emphasized the specificity of the facilitating effects of propranolol on the expression of the orienting reaction.

6) Patients receiving propranolol and phenothiazines together resembled the normal volunteers more than they did the untreated patients or those on either drug alone with respect to the resting skin conductance as well as the amplitude of the orienting reaction and its bilateral symmetry and rate of habituation.

7) The data suggest that the abnormalities in neural mechanisms that underlie the control of expression of autonomic orienting processes and their habituation in schizophrenia may

be, at least partially, corrected by the administration of propranolol alone and even more effectively when propranolol is given with phenothiazines. Phenothiazines alone appear to be ineffective.

REFERENCES

1. Yorkston NJ, Zaki SA, Themen JFA, Havard CWH: Early observations on the effect of propranolol on psychotic patients. Adv Clin Pharmacol 12:91, 1976.
2. Yorkston NJ, Gruzelier JH, Zaki SA, Hollander D, Pitcher DR, Sergeant HGS: Effects of adding propranolol to the treatment of schizophrenic patients who had not responded to major tranquillisers: A controlled study. The Lancet ii:575–578, 1977.
3. Yorkston NJ, Zaki SA, Malik MKU, Morrison RC, Havard CWH: Propranolol in the control of schziophrenic symptoms. Br Med J 4:633, 1974.
4. Lykken DR, Venables PH: Direct measurement of skin conductance: A proposal for standardisation. Psychophysiology 8:656, 1972.
5. Gruzelier JH, Hammond NV: The effect of chlorpromazine upon bilateral asymmetries of bioelectrical skin reactivity in schizophrenia. Stud Psychol 19:40, 1977.
6. Gruzelier JH, Hammond NV: The effect of chlorpromazine on psychophysiological, endocrine and information processing measures in schizophrenia. J Psychiatr Res (In press).
7. Gruzelier JH, Venables PH: Skin conductance orienting activity in a heterogenous sample of schizophrenics: Possible evidence of limbic dysfunction. J Nerv Ment Dis 155:277, 1972.
8. Gruzelier JH, Venables PH: Bimodality and lateral asymmetry of skin conductance orienting activity in schizophrenics: Replication and evidence of lateral asymmetry in patients with depression and disorders of personality. Biol Psychiatry 8:55, 1974.
9. Gruzelier JH: Bilateral asymmetry of skin conductance orienting activity and levels in schizophrenia. J Biol Psychol 1:21, 1973.
10. Gruzelier JH, Hammond NV: Schizophrenia: A dominant hemisphere temporal-limbic disorder? Res Commun Psychol Psychiatr Behav 1:33, 1976.
11. Bagshaw MH, Benzier S: Multiple measures of the orienting reaction and their dissociation after amygdalectomy in monkeys. Exp Neurol 20:175, 1968.
12. Patterson T: Skin conductance responding/non-responding and pupillometrics in chronic schizophrenia: A confirmation of Gruzelier and Venables. J Nerv Ment Dis 163:200, 1976.
13. Straube E: Personal communication.

14. Groves PM, Thompson RF: Habituation: A dual-process theory. Psychol Rev 77:419, 1970.
15. Lader MH, Wing L: "Physiological Measures, Sedative Drugs, and Morbid Anxiety." Institute of Psychiatry. Maudsley Monographs 14. London: Oxford University Press.
16. Uherik A: Interpretation of bilateral asymmetry of bioelectrical skin reactivity in schizophrenics. Stud Psychol 17:51, 1975.
17. Gruzelier JH: Bimodal arousal and lateralised dysfunction in schizophrenia: The effect of chlorpromazine on psychophysiological, information processing and endocrine measures. In Wynne L, Cromwell R, Matthysse E (eds): "Nature of Schizophrenia: New Findings and Future Strategies." New York: Wiley, 1977.
18. Lacey JI: Somatic response patterning and stress: Some revisions of activation theory. In Appley MH, Trumball R (eds): "Psychological Stress: Issues in Research." New York: Appleton-Century-Crofts, 1967.
19. Gruzelier JH, Venables PH: Skin conductance responses to tones with and without attentional significance in schizophrenic and non-schizophrenic patients. Neuropsychologia 11:221, 1973.
20. Raskin DC: Attention and arousal. In Prokasy WF, Raskin DC (eds): "Electrodermal Activity in Psychological Research." New York: Academic Press.
21. Bohlin G: Delayed habituation of the electrodermal orienting response as a function of increased level of arousal. Psychophysiology 13:345, 1976.
22. Richardson JS: Basic concepts of psychopharmacological research as applied to the psychopharmacological analysis of the amygdala. Acta Neurobiol Exp 34:543, 1974.
23. Eleftheriou BF (ed): "The Neurobiology of the Amygdala." New York: Plenum Press, 1972.
24. Pribram KH, McGuiness D: Arousal, activation and effort in the control of attention. Psychol Rev 82:116, 1975.
25. Atsmon A, Blum I, Fischl J: Treatment of an acute attak of porphyria variegata with propranolol. S Afr Med J 46:311, 1972.
26. Atsmon A, Blum I: The discovery. This volume pp 5–38.

4. Does Thought Flow Relate to Blood Flow?

Eugene Roberts

Increased functional demands in various regions of the brain result in increased metabolism in them and in a consequent increase in blood flow. Although the exact mechanisms of the coordinations between the two processes are not known, there is a coupling between function, metabolism, and blood flow probably not different in principle from that which exists in other regions of the body. Pertinent data and relevant techniques have been discussed in a recent symposium (1).

Perhaps of greatest interest in the present context have been the observations showing there to be an abnormal distribution of cerebral blood flow (rCBF) in chronic schizophrenics measured by a technique employing radioactive xenon clearance monitored by computer-operated multiple detectors placed on the scalp overlying the left (dominant) hemispheres of conscious individuals (2). This technique gives "functional landscapes" that reflect brain activity (3). Quoting from the former reference, "It was confirmed that the mean hemisphere blood flow was normal. The rCBF distribution was, however, significantly abnormal with low flows frontally and high flows postcentrally, instead of the opposite. The 'hypofrontal' rCBF pattern could not be explained on the basis of age, somatic factors, or medication, but appeared specific to schizophrenia. Several significant correlations were found between the RP-ratings

Propranolol and Schizophrenia, pages 119–123

(Rockland-Pollin scale) and the rCBF findings. The lower the frontal flow the more inactive, indifferent and autistic were the patients. The higher the postcentral flows, the more pronounced was the cognitive disturbance of the patients." The authors caution that, "Both the abnormal flow (activity) distribution and the psychic symptoms may indeed be two paraphenomena of a third, or indeed several, as yet unknown abnormalities in the brain which may underlie the schizophrenic disorder."

The above procedure is difficult to apply, entails some hazards for the patient, and has limited resolution. However, a newly developed technique, positron-emission transaxial tomography, that employs intravenous injections of tracer doses of short-lived positron-emitting substances such as ^{11}CO-hemoglobin, $^{13}NH_3$, or ^{18}F-labeled deoxyglucose provides a safe, new method for imaging quantitatively the hemodynamic and metabolic functions of the brain as well as the other organs in conscious individuals at a high level of resolution (4–6). The development of the latter technique now has created the opportunity to perform serial studies, so that patients undergoing treatment with propranolol or other drugs can be followed longitudinally from before treatment to determine whether or not any correlation exists between recovery in some of them and specific alterations in regional metabolic or blood flow patterns. If correlations should be found, it might be possible to determine whether the psychiatric improvement precedes or follows the physiologic changes. The answer to this question could have important practical and theoretical implications. Employing the above technique, questions about correlative functional activities of the various extracerebral tissues also could be asked at little additional cost. The latter might not necessarily be irrelevant, since it is not established that pertinent disturbances in schizophrenic disorders reside only in the central nervous system.

Until such data as discussed above become available, we must content ourselves with work in animals. Experiments with baboons indicate that stimulation of central adrenergic receptors by exogenous administration or endogenous release of norepinephrine leads to an increase in overall cerebral metabolism, and that secondarily there is an increase in cerebral circulation (6–9). Ordinarily, norepinephrine does not pass the blood-brain barrier readily, but in those instances when it does, low concentrations of it cause increased cerebral blood flow, cerebral oxygen consumption, and cerebral glucose uptake (7). This raises the question as to whether or not there may be temporary or permanent regional impairment in the barrier to the entry of norepinephrine and other normally excluded circulating neuroactive substances in schizophrenic individuals. In this regard, it is interesting that propranolol produced an immediate, significant reduction in both cerebral oxygen consumption and cerebral glucose uptake in normal baboons (8), suggesting that brain metabolism can be altered importantly by blockade of β-adrenergic receptors.

Although not able to attend our conference because of prior commitments, L. Sokoloff was stimulated to study the effects of propranolol and of phentolamine, an α-adrenergic blocking agent, on regional cerebral metabolism in the rat, employing his elegant autoradiographic technique following the injection of 2-[^{14}C]-deoxyglucose (10, 11). He has given us permission to quote from an abstract of a paper to be presented at the 1977 meeting of the Society of Neuroscience (12). "Normal conscious rats were infused intravenously with 0.25, 0.5, or 1.0 mg/kg/min of propranolol or 0.25, 0.5, or 0.83 mg/kg/min of phentolamine. Forty minutes after the administration of the drug, local cerebral glucose utilization was measured during a 45-min period. Propranolol caused dose-dependent reductions in cerebral glucose utilization in several regions of brain, most prominently in the structures of the auditory pathway. Phentolamine also caused local reductions of cerebral glucose utilization in a number of cerebral structures but, in contrast to propranolol, caused increases in glucose consumption in the auditory system. These results suggest that adrenergic synapses may play an important role in the function of the auditory pathway in the rat."

One immediately can ask the question as to whether the above observations may be related to the clinical reports in this volume stating that one of the prominent features of propranolol administration to schizophrenic patients is the amelioration of auditory hallucinations.

Metabolic effects of norepinephrine and propranolol can be exerted via action on β-receptors located on neurons, glia, and blood vessels in the brain. An active field of investigation at the present time, and one that may be particularly pertinent to the problems considered at this conference, deals with the effects of norepinephrine and other neurotransmitter candidates on cerebral blood vessels. This is the subject of the following chapter.

REFERENCES

1. Ingvar DH, Lassen NA (eds): "Brain Work. The Coupling of Function, Metabolism and Blood Flow in the Brain." New York: Academic Press, 1975.
2. Franzén G, Ingvar DH: Abnormal distribution of cerebral activity in chronic schizophrenia. J Psychiatr Res 12:199–214, 1975.
3. Ingvar DH: Functional landscapes of the dominant hemisphere. Brain Res 107:181–197, 1976.
4. Phelps ME, Hoffman EJ, Mullani NA, Ter-Pogossian MM: Application of annihilation coincidence detection to transaxial reconstruction tomography. J Nuclear Med 16:210–224, 1975.
5. Hoffman EJ, Phelps ME, Mullani NA, Higgins CS, Ter-Pogossian MM: Design and performance characteristics of a whole-body positron transaxial tomograph. J Nuclear Med 17:493–502, 1976.
6. Phelps ME, Hoffman EJ, Coleman RE, Welch MJ, Raichle ME, Weiss ES, Sobel BE, Ter-Pogossian MM: Tomographic images of blood pool and perfusion in brain and heart. J Nuclear Med 17:603–612, 1976.
7. MacKenzie ET, McCulloch J, O'Keane M, Pickard JD, Harper AM: Cerebral circulation and norepinephrine: relevance of the blood-brain barrier. Am J Physiol 231:483–488, 1976.
8. MacKenzie ET, McCulloch J, Harper AM: Influence of endogenous norepinephrine on cerebral blood flow and metabolism. Am J Physiol 231:489–494, 1976.
9. McCulloch J, Harper AM: Cerebral circulatory and metabolism changes following amphetamine administration. Brain Res 121:196–199, 1977.

10. Kennedy C, Des Rosiers MH, Jehle JW, Reivich M, Sharp F, Sokoloff L: Mapping of functional neural pathways by autoradiographic survey of local metabolic rate with [C^{14}]-deoxyglucose technique. Science 187:850–853, 1975.
11. Kennedy C, Des Rosiers MH, Sakurada O, Shinohara M, Reivich M, Jehle JW, Sokoloff L: Metabolic mapping of primary visual system of monkey by means of autoradiographic [C^{14}]-deoxyglucose technique. Proc Natl Acad Sci USA 73:4230–4234, 1976.
12. Savaki H, Kadekaro M, Sokoloff L: Effects of propranolol and phentolamine on local cerebral glucose utilization in the rat. Abstract, 1977 Meeting, Society for Neuroscience.

5. Blood Vessels in the Brain Also Have Nerves

Amine-Mediated Vasomotor Functions in Cranial Vessels

Lars Edvinsson, J. E. Hardebo, and Ch. Owman

INTRODUCTION

Detailed knowledge about amine receptor functions in, for example, the coronary, renal, and mesenteric vascular beds has formed the basis for our understanding of various types of circulatory control functions and pathophysiological mechanisms, as well as for a rational pharmacological approach to the clinical treatment of some important cardiovascular disorders. Such basic information has for a long time been lacking for the cerebral circulation, mainly because it has been a generally accepted idea – and it is, unfortunately, still believed by some – that brain vessels are unique in being devoid of nerves, and hence that the control of cerebral blood flow is exerted entirely via metabolic factors, such as changes in the arterial CO_2 tension and extracellular pH. This misconception is partly due to previous lack of histological methods for unequivocal demonstration of perivascular nerves in the brain, and it has been further perpetuated by certain electron-microscopic reports in which the investigators either could not find any nerves at all in relation to small brain vessels (1), or could only demonstrate such nerve fibers running at the surface of the blood vessels without penetrating deeper into the smooth muscular media (2). This is particularly unfortunate since we know that a negative electron-microscopic observation usually is of little value because of the

Propranolol and Schizophrenia, pages 125–147

extremely small areas of sectioned tissue preparation that become available for analysis at the high resolution required, and since we know today that the localization of nerves only at the surface of the blood vessel is, in fact, the characteristic organization of a vascular autonomic innervation. There have, of course, been a number of physiological observations indicating that the brain circulation might be influenced by neurogenic mechanisms, but with the very meager structural basis for such mechanisms it has often been thought that positive results were artifacts of the experimental situation caused by variables beyond the control of the investigator.

CEREBROVASCULAR INNERVATION

With the introduction more than a decade ago of new neurohistochemical techniques possessing a unique degree of sensitivity and specificity (3), it became possible to show that the cerebrovascular bed receives an extensive sympathetic innervation, which in some regions is better developed than in most other vascular beds. It has since been shown that the cerebral vessels are directly reached by several different systems of nerve terminals not only of extracranial (such as the sympathetics) but probably also of intracranial origin. Apart from these more easily definable pathways, the cerebral blood flow may also be changed in response to altered activity of the extensively distributed aminergic systems running within the brain, directly or via hitherto unknown mediators.

Most of the studies on the cerebrovascular innervation have so far been focused on autonomic nerves (4). Thus, a well-developed system of adrenergic fibers originating in the superior cervical sympathetic ganglia supplies the pial vascular bed as well as the intracerebral system of resistance vessels. The sympathetic supply of vessels belonging to the carotid system is more extensive than that of the vertebral system. A considerable heterogeneity has been found with regard to the number of arterioles receiving adrenergic terminals in the brain parenchyma, as illustrated in Fig. 1. There is direct experimental evidence suggesting that this regional heterogeneity in the amount of cerebrovascular innervation

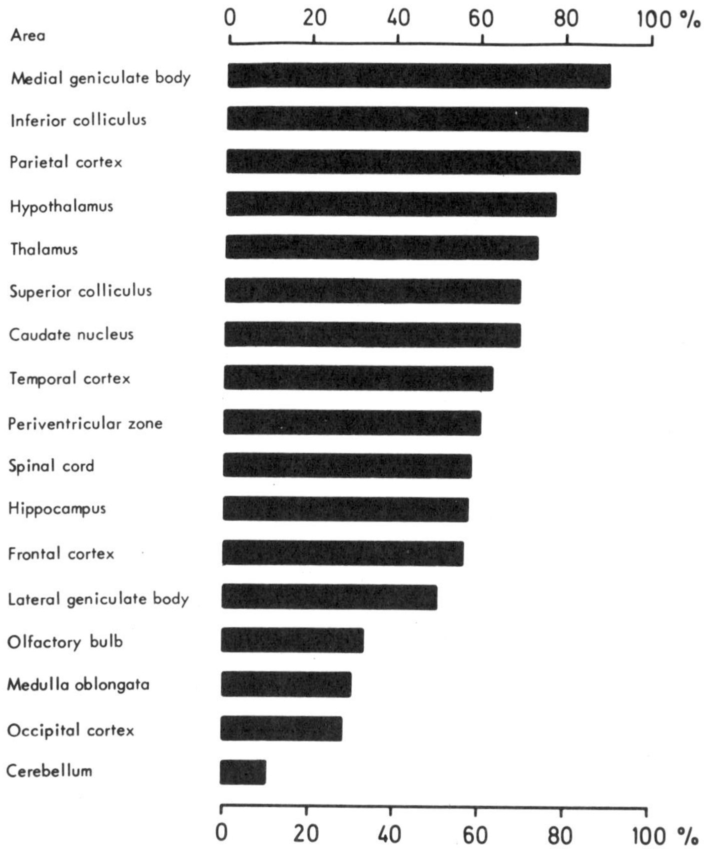

Fig. 1. Fluorescence microscopic evaluation of the percentage of arterioles in various brain regions of baboons supplied by adrenergic sympathetic nerves, visualized in sections from formaldehyde-treated tissue preparations.

may be directly related to the degree of vasomotor reaction that can be evoked by sympathetic nerve stimulation or by the administration of sympathomimetic amines (5).

The cerebrovascular sympathetic nerves are accompanied by an equally well-developed system of fibers (not affected by sympathectomy) containing specific acetylcholinesterase (as evidenced by histochemical staining in conjunction with specific inhibitors) and, therefore, designated as cholinergic (6). The origin of these fibers is not fully known, but many of them appear to run in the facial nerve and to turn off in the region of the geniculate ganglion to continue in the greater superficial petrosal nerve to the plexus of the internal carotid artery, where they form synapses.* In the pial vascular system, the plexuses of adrenergic and cholinergic axon terminals are closely related to one another, with a membrane-to-membrane distance of only 25 nm, forming the structural basis for an axoaxonal interaction (see further below). It should be noted that, so far, cholinesterase-positive fibers have been found only in association with the pial vascular systems, whereas the intracerebral vessels seem to be devoid of such nerves (although it cannot be fully excluded that this simply reflects the relatively low sensitivity of the histochemical technique for demonstration of acetylcholinesterase).

Recently, quite another system of nerve fibers has been visualized by the immunohistochemical demonstration of "vasoactive intestinal polypeptide" (VIP) (7). The axons have principally the same relationship to brain vessels as the adrenergic nerves, but cervical sympathetic ganglionectomy has shown that the VIP-containing fibers have another origin; they may even arise from intracerebral sources. Preliminary tests under in vitro conditions suggest that the VIP system exerts vasodilatory effects also in brain vessels (7). It is thus not unlikely that the VIP nerves may be involved in the non-adrenergic, noncholinergic cerebral vasodilatory mechanism suggested by the studies of Lee et al. (8).

Intracerebral noradrenergic nerves, originating in the locus coeruleus and adjacent regions, have a close association with intracerebral arterioles (9), and it has therefore been implicated that this widespread system may have a direct influence on cerebral microcirculation (10). There is experimental evidence to support this assumption, but since there

*There is some evidence in the literature that the intracranial arteries are also supplied with afferent nerve fibers. The amount of acetylcholinesterase in this type of nerve appears to be so low that substantial staining is obtained only after prolonged incubation. This would mean that acetylcholinesterase staining under conditions such as those employed in our studies on brain vessels only reveals the efferent (parasympathetic) fibers.

also are indications from denervation studies in conjunction with electron microscopy that only the above-mentioned sympathetic terminals innervate intracerebral arterioles in a true sense, we then have to assume some kind of long-distance diffusion of transmitter from the intracerebral noradrenaline neurons to the vascular smooth muscle. This, may in fact, be the process by which the other systems of intracerebral nerves affect cerebral blood flow – unless, as mentioned above, some kind of second mediator is involved.

Nonmyelinated nerve fibers of unknown origin, resembling autonomic axons and containing a majority of moderately electron-dense synaptic vesicles, also innervate capillary pericytes and endothelial cells in the hypothalamus, as shown by electron microscopy (11). This has interesting implications in view of the recent finding that immunohistochemically visible contractile proteins (actin and myosin) are present in the cytoplasm of both types of cells (12). It may provide a mechanism for a neurogenic vasomotor control also at the capillary level and/or it may underlie the changes in permeability of the blood-brain barrier that can be induced by sympathetic nerve stimulation (13).

CONTRACTILE RECEPTOR FUNCTION IN CRANIAL VESSELS

Release of noradrenaline from the sympathetic nerves of brain vessels, either induced by administration of an indirectly acting sympathomimetic amine, such as tyramine (14), or by electrical stimulation of the perivascular nerves (15), produces vasoconstriction. The sympathetic nerve stimulation is associated with a reduction in local cerebral blood flow, provided the brain region in which the measurements are made has a sufficiently well developed adrenergic innervation of its resistance vessels (5). For this reason, primary pharmacological interest has been directed to the cerebral vasoconstriction mediated by the sympathetic neurotransmitter noradrenaline and related sympathomimetic amines. The potency ratio for such amines in their contractile effects, together with the mode of inhibition caused by specific reversible or irreversible competitive inhibitors, has shown that the vasoconstriction is mediated by α-receptors (16).

The affinity of noradrenaline for the α-receptors, expressed in terms of the dissociation constant K_A which is obtained after irreversible inhibition of a fraction of the receptors, resembles that found for the rat portal vein, but is slightly lower than that reported for the rabbit aortic strip (16). The relation between the actual noradrenaline-induced response and the α-receptor occupancy showed that the contraction is not directly proportional to the fraction of receptors occupied. Half-maximum contraction of the vessel (ED_{50}) is achieved with only about 11% of the receptors occupied, and maximum contraction (E_{Am}) is reached when about 75% are occupied by noradrenaline (Fig. 2a).

When pH is increased (without changing pCO_2) in the medium in which the test artery is suspended, the response to a given dose of noradrenaline is markedly enhanced (Fig. 2b), whereas a reduced degree of contraction is obtained at pH levels below normal (17). Alterations of pCO_2 levels (at constant pH) had little or no effect on the cerebrovascular reactivity to noradrenaline. These observations support the idea that perivascular pH, rather than pCO_2, is of primary importance in the so-called metabolic regulation of the vessel diameter. It is suggested that the mechanism of action of pH may involve, at least in part, the sympathetic neuroeffector apparatus by modulating the vasomotor action of noradrenaline at the α-receptors. The exact localization of the pH effect is difficult to determine, but it seems probable that it is partly involved in the excitation-contraction coupling process (17). In view of the relatively large modifications of active tension produced by relatively small changes in pH, and since blood flow varies with the fourth power of vessel radius, it seems likely that such an interaction may play a significant role in the local regulation of cerebral blood flow.

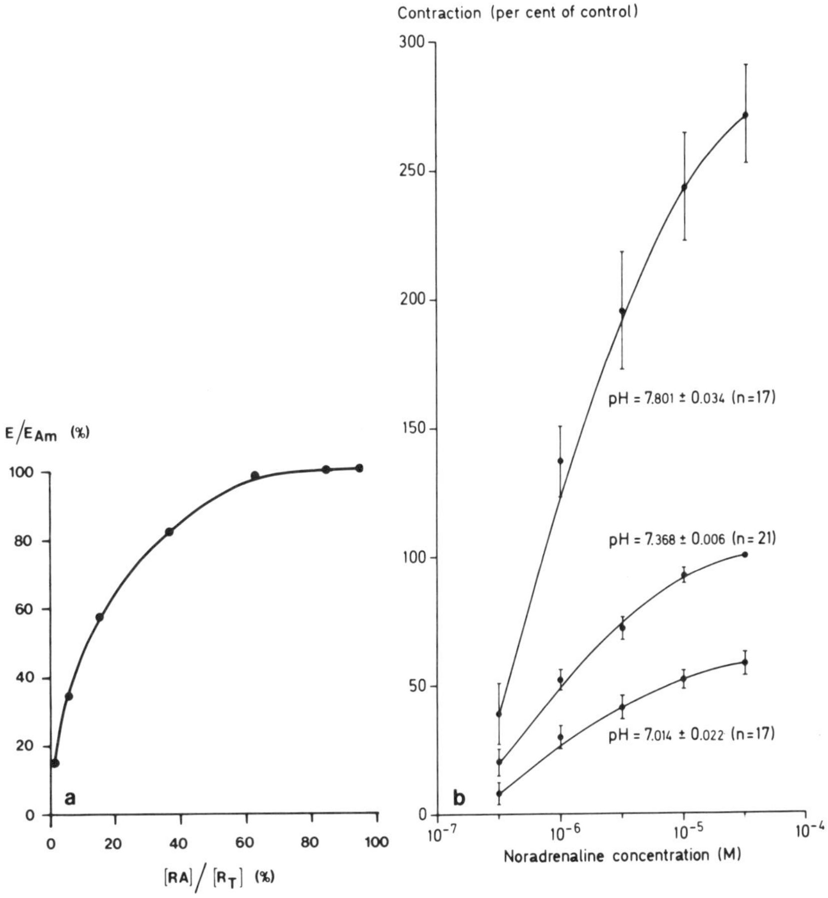

Fig. 2. α-Receptor response in isolated middle cerebral artery from cat tested under in vitro conditions. (a) Relation between actual contractile response and fractional receptor occupancy. E, Effect obtained after noradrenaline administration; E_{Am}, maximum response; [RA], concentration of the complex between α-receptor and noradrenaline; [RT], total concentration of α-receptors. (b) Dose-response relation of noradrenaline at different pH values of the Krebs-Ringer buffer solution. The experiments were performed on sympathectomized or cocaine-treated (10^{-6}M) vessels (to avoid neuronal uptake), in the presence of normetanephrine (to inhibit extraneuronal uptake) and propranolol (to block dilatory β-receptors). The pH was changed by adding small quantities of 0.1 N HCl or 1.0 N NaOH at constant pCO_2. Values are mean ± SEM; number of experiments within parentheses.

There is reason to believe that the α-receptor present in the intracranial vasculature differs from α-receptors in peripheral smooth musculature. The dissociation constant for the receptor-antagonist complex (K_B) does not conform with corresponding values for such smooth muscle tissues; the ED_{50} values for sympathomimetic amines are comparatively high, particularly for phenylephrine which, moreover, only acts as a partial agonist in the intracranial vascular bed (16).

Within 3 days after sympathetic denervation of the brain vessels, an approximately threefold increase in the sensitivity to noradrenaline develops (14). A similar degree of supersensitivity is seen (in innervated vessels) with cocaine, supporting the prejunctional nature of this phenomenon. It has recently been found in rabbits that pial vessels also achieve an increased sensitivity to noradrenaline of the same magnitude within 3 days after a cisternal injection of autologous blood (18). This change in reactivity is associated with a reduction in the content of noradrenaline of the perivascular nerves, and an impairment of the mechanism for transmitter uptake. These findings have led to the assumption that a prejunctional type of receptor supersensitivity to noradrenaline develops in conjunction with a subarachnoid hemorrhage and may be involved in the development and maintenance of the associated cerebral vasospasm (19).

Numerous investigations have been concerned with the cerebrovascular effects of histamine, particularly because of the clinical relevance of the problem. A number of conflicting results have been obtained with histamine, from no alteration in cerebral blood flow to strong vasoconstriction, or to a vasodilation. It has even been suggested that the action of histamine on cerebral blood flow has reflected artifacts related to effects on the extracranial circulation, systemic effects, or to actions on vascular permeability. This confusing situation, together with the recent observation that mast cells in the brain often have a perivascular localization, sometimes with a distance to the arteriolar smooth musculature of only 20 nm (20) (Fig. 3), has stimulated a more detailed pharmacological analysis of the histamine receptors under standardized in vitro situations (21). Under these conditions, histamine produces

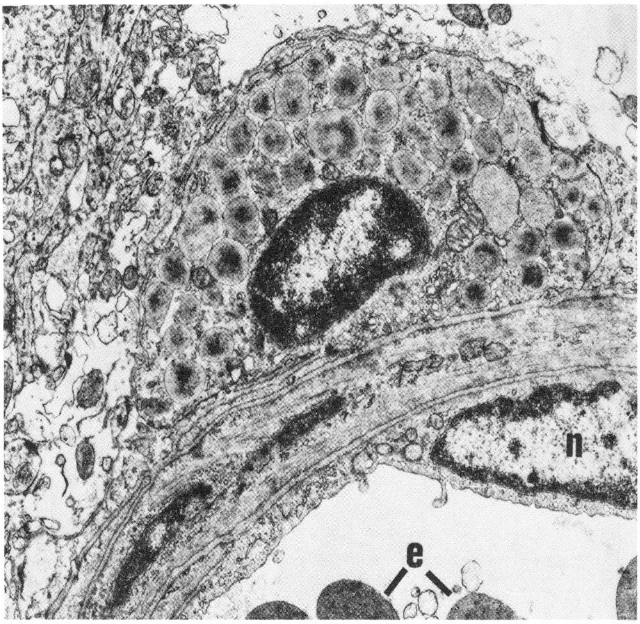

Fig. 3. Electron micrograph of mast cell abutting on the wall of a small intracerebral arteriole of a cat. There is a close relationship between the membranes of the mast cell and the underlying muscle cell, the gap being only some 20 nm wide and occupied by the fused basement membranes. n, Nucleus of endothelial cell; e, erythrocytes. × 5,000.

both vasodilation (see below) and vasoconstriction (Fig. 4). In extracranial arteries (branches from the external maxillary or lingual arteries), the vasoconstriction produced by histamine is quite remarkable with an ED_{50} value that is only one-tenth of that found for intracranial arteries (middle cerebral artery used as model). The maximum contraction obtained in the latter was only about one-third of that seen with extracranial arteries. The response of the extracranial vessels was inhibited in a competitive manner with increasing doses of mepyramine, showing that the contractile effect was mediated by the H_1 type of receptors. The mean K_B value was found to be of the same order of magnitude as those previously reported for other tissues. In the intracranial vessels, however, both of the specific H_1 receptor antagonists tested, mepyramine and chlorpheniramine, produced a reduction in the slope of the

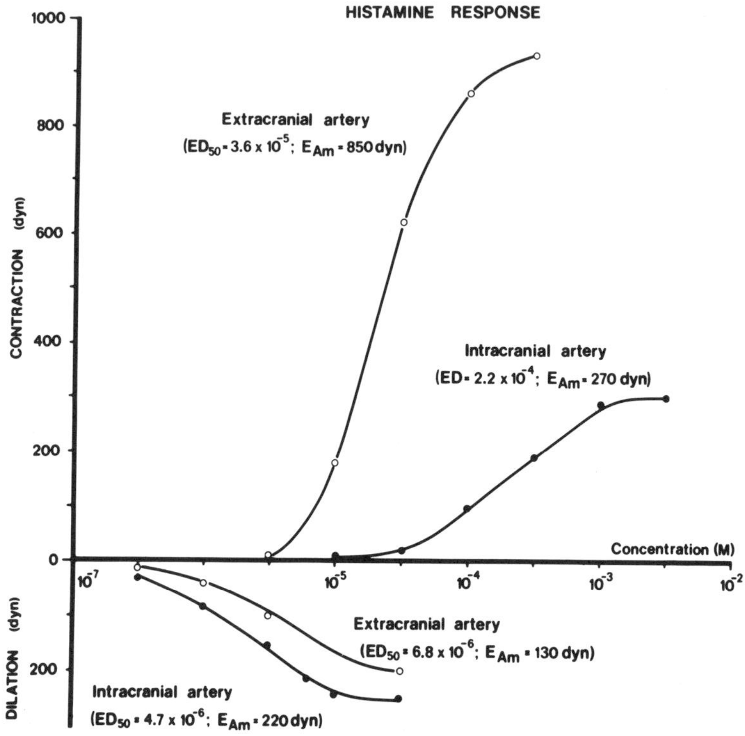

Fig. 4. Composite picture of representative curves comparing the effects of histamine on feline intra- and extracranial arteries in vitro. Contractile responses were obtained with the H_2 receptors blocked, and dilatory effects were recorded during blockade of the contractile H_1 receptors and with the vessel starting at an active tonic contraction of some 250 dyne by the presence of 3×10^{-6} M 5-HT.

dose-response curve and in the maximum effect of histamine, suggesting that the contractile effect on the vascular smooth muscles in these vessels is of a nonspecific nature. Obviously, this emphasizes the importance of testing the vasomotor actions of any biogenic amine in full dose-response curves, prior to and after addition of various specific antagonists, before a conclusion can be drawn about the type of receptors mediating a particular response. The results also suggest that histamine-induced vasoconstriction in the brain may have more of a pharmacological than a physiological interest.

It has been suggested that 5-hydroxytryptamine (5-HT), released from blood platelets after a subarachnoid hemorrhage, might be involved as a pathophysiological factor in the development of the associated cerebral vasospasm (10). We have known for a long time (22) that 5-HT is a potent vasoconstrictor amine for brain vessels, and it has been shown that sufficient concentrations may occur in human cerebrospinal fluid following subarachnoid hemorrhage and in serum to produce a strong contraction of brain vessels (23). From a clinical viewpoint there is much evidence suggesting that 5-HT is also involved in the etiology of migraine.

Reports are conflicting concerning the effect of 5-HT on the intra- and extracranial circulation. Thus, a reduction of the cerebral blood flow and a large increment of the extracranial blood flow have been measured. On the other hand, some investigators have observed a reduction in both intra- and extracranial blood flow. Since all of these experiments have utilized complicated in vivo models, it is not possible to decide whether the responses have been specific in the sense that they have involved specific 5-HT receptors in the vascular wall. A quantitative phamacological characterization of the receptors mediating the 5-HT-induced vasomotor response has, therefore, been carried out on isolated vascular segments from cat and man in vitro, comparing the responses in vascular segments from the intra- and extracranial vascular beds simultaneously under identical conditions (24). The potency rank for the contractile response was the same in intra- and extracranial arteries, in the order 5-HT = LSD (d-lysergic acid diethylamide) > tryptamine. One difficulty in the pharmacological characterization of vascular responses being mediated by specific 5-HT receptors is the lack of sufficiently well-defined 5-HT receptor antagonists. Available substances influence not only the 5-HT receptors but, to a varying degree, also adrenergic, cholinergic, and histaminergic receptors. Hence, they have only a narrow dose range in which the antagonism can be regarded as specific for one or the other of these receptors. Methysergide has been shown to be a specific 5-HT receptor antagonist on smooth muscle (25), and its effect on adrenergic receptors is, at least in vitro, negligible. Furthermore, methysergide does not interfere with the smooth muscle effects of acetylcholine and histamine and has, like other lysergic acid derivatives, a structural similarity to 5-HT. Structurally, LSD resembles methysergide and is commonly used as a 5-HT antagonist. Methysergide produced a parallel shift of the dose-response curves toward higher concentrations of 5-HT, and the calculated pA_2 value for the interaction between 5-HT and this antagonist agreed with those reported from experiments on rabbit aorta and rat fundus strips (24). It has been suggested that part of the contractile 5-HT effect might involve stimulation of α-adrenergic receptors. However, moderate concentrations of the α-antagonist, phentolamine, which was shown to produce a clear parallel shift in the dose-response curve of noradrenaline (16), did not affect the constriction induced by 5-HT. Phenoxybenzamine, an irreversible α-antagonist, tested in a dose that completely abolished the noradrenaline response, only slightly reduced the 5-HT effect. We, therefore, conclude that 5-HT mediates its contractile effect on extracranial arteries via specific 5-HT receptors. In both cat and man, the intracranial vessels were found to be more sensitive than the extracranial ones to 5-HT. The contractile effect of 5-HT on intracranial vessels was also inhibited by methysergide, but the inhibition involved a reduction in the maximum contraction and the slope of the dose-response curve. The antagonistic effect was reversible in the sense that it was easily eliminated by washing. As for the extracranial arteries, α-receptor antagonists had little or no effect on the response. The results showing that the potency rank for 5-HT and related agonists is the same in both types of vessels indicate that a 5-HT receptor also is involved in contraction of the intracranial arteries. However, the intracranial arteries are more sensitive to 5-HT than the extracranial ones, and there seem to be other differences with regard to the receptor in the two types of vessels (24).

With regard to the possible role of 5-HT in the pathophysiology of cerebral vasospasm following subarachnoid hemorrhage, the sensitivity of rabbit pial arteries to 5-HT was studied 3 days after cisternal injection of autologous blood to simulate subarachnoid bleeding (18). When tested on the basilar artery in vitro, 5-HT produced approximately threefold stronger contraction of the vessel from rabbits receiving the cisternal blood injection when compared with arteries from control animals (Fig. 5). The mechanism does not seem to involve the sympathetic nervous system, since removal of the superior cervical ganglion has no influence on the reactivity of the cerebral arteries to 5-HT. The results agree with the idea that 5-HT is somehow involved in the pathogenesis of cerebral vascular spasm, which corroborates the observations that blood from dogs pretreated with reserpine, which is known to inhibit the accumulation of 5-HT in the blood platelets and thus reduce their 5-HT concentration, failed to produce spasm when injected into the subarachnoid space of normal dogs (26).

DILATORY RECEPTOR FUNCTIONS IN CRANIAL VESSELS

A sympathomimetic dilatory response is easily obtained in isolated brain vessels under conditions when the contractile α-receptor is inhibited (by, e.g., phenoxybenzamine) and – if a high degree of dilatation already prevails under the experimental conditions used – after the vessel has tonically contracted (by, e.g., 5-HT, KCl, prostaglandin $F_{2\alpha}$). The relative potency for drugs producing dilatory response has been found to be in the order isoproterenol > noradrenaline = adrenaline > terbutaline (16). The effect is inhibited in a competitive way by propranolol (16) and practolol (27), showing that β-receptor is involved, and the pA_2 values obtained agree with those reported for other isolated tissues (28). From the finding that isoproterenol was 2,500 times more potent than terbutaline in its dilatory action, and that the potency ratio for noradrenaline to adrenaline was 1.2:1, it was concluded that the β-receptor is of the β_1-type. Further support for the view that the cerebrovascular β-receptor should be classified as a β_1-type has recently been obtained under in vivo conditions, where changes in local blood flow of the caudate nucleus in nonanesthetized rabbits were

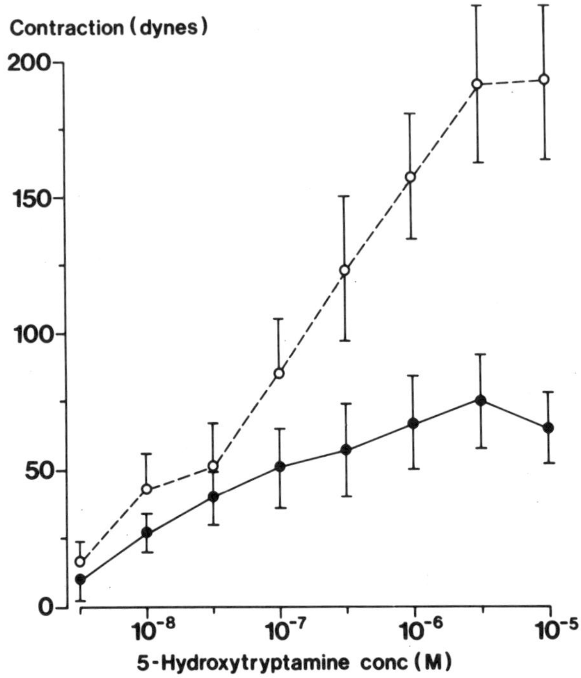

Fig. 5. Dose-response curves showing the increased in vitro sensitivity to 5-HT in arteries from rabbits with 1.0 ml of intracisternal blood 3 days before the test (open circles) as compared with normal basilar arteries (filled circles). The curves represent values of mean ± SEM from tests on arteries from 10 animals.

followed by the thermoclearance technique (27). As illustrated in Fig. 6, isoproterenol increased the caudate blood flow and reduced systemic blood pressure. The β_2-receptor agonist terbutaline, on the other hand, had only systemic effects. The caudate nucleus flow response was selectively blocked by the β_1-receptor antagonist practolol, whereas propranolol inhibited all effects (central as well as systemic) of both agonists. This would mean that the β-receptor in the brain vessels resembles those of the coronary circulation, whereas other parts of the peripheral vascular bed seem to possess the β_2-type of receptors. This is supported by the fact that the potency ratio for the dilatory response induced by isoproternol and terbutaline in extracranial arteries is only approximately 100:1.

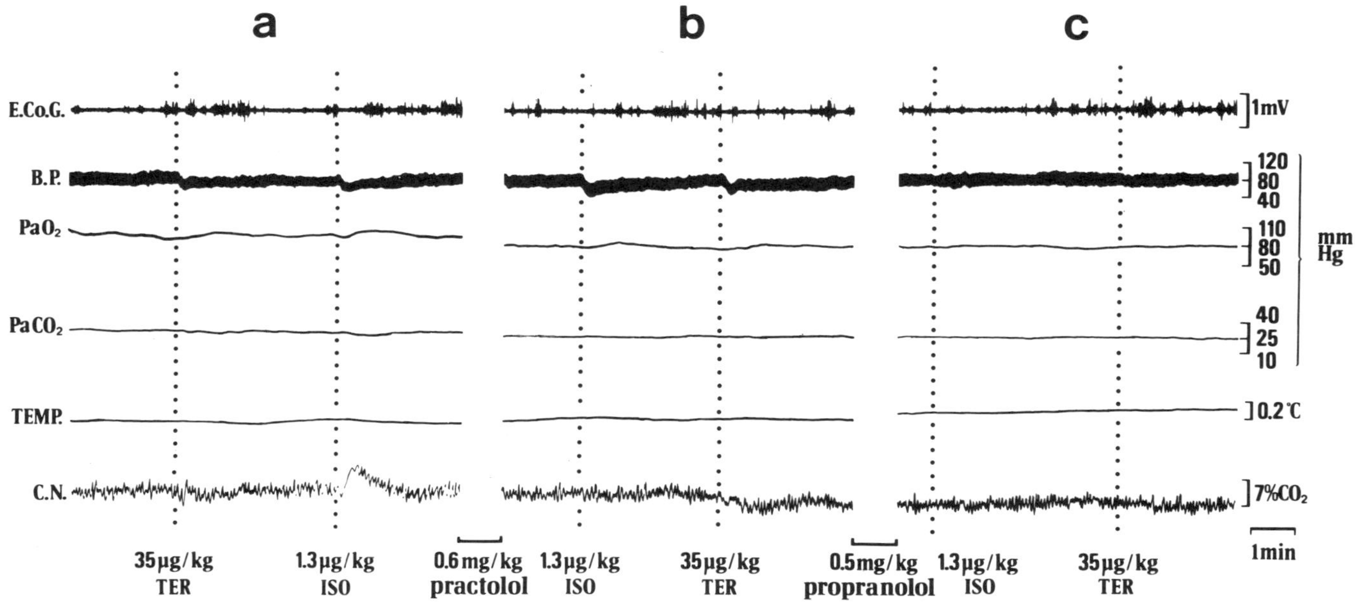

Fig. 6. Representative experiments performed by the thermoclearance technique in a nonanesthetized rabbit, illustrating different effects of isoproterenol (ISO) and terbutaline (TER) on the blood flow in the caudate nucleus (C.N.), on the arterial blood pressure (B.P.), and on associated variables. E.Co.G., Electrocorticogram; $PaCO_2$ and PaO_2, partial pressure of CO_2 and O_2 in the aorta; TEMP., temperature in the caudate nucleus on opposite side of flow measurement. The calibration is indicated to the right (a) B.P. is reduced after addition of the two agonists in nontreated animals, whereas only isoproterenol increases the caudate nucleus blood flow. (b) Practolol inhibits only the cerebral vascular response to isoproterenol, whereas (c) propranolol abolishes all effects.

The cholinergic vasodilation in the brain provides a particularly complex problem since it involves both postjunctional actions on the vascular smooth musculature and prejunctional effects mediated by the above-mentioned axoaxonal relationship between the adrenergic and cholinergic perivascular nerves (6). In isolated middle cerebral arteries (previously given an active tonic constriction) acetylcholine and carbamylcholine produce a dose-dependent dilatation in concentrations up to a level of 10^{-6} M. The response is inhibited in a competitive manner by atropine, showing that the effect is mediated by the muscarinic type of cholinergic receptor (29). At high doses, above 10^{-6} M, acetylcholine produces a dose-dependent contraction, and this effect, too, is inhibited in a competitive manner with atropine. It may be assumed that the dilatory effect, occurring in the lower dose range, is the physiologically more relevant response, which agrees with observations that increased cerebral blood flow is obtained with parasympathomimetic compounds under in vivo conditions. The experiments performed on sympathectomized vessels would thus indicate the presence of a direct cholinergic vasodilator receptor mechanism in the pial system. The salivary glands represent another example of a vascular bed where the vasodilation does not occur only through inhibition of the sympathetic vasoconstrictor fibers (30).

The close relationship between the perivascular adrenergic and cholinergic axon varicosities in the pial arteries (6) suggested that the cholinergic system might influence not only the vascular smooth muscle cells, but also adjacent adrenergic axons in the neuroeffector area. Indeed, it was found (29) that the release of noradrenaline from the perivascular nerves of pial vessels during transmural electrical stimulation in vitro was inhibited by acetylcholine or nicotine, whereas the spontaneous release of noradrenaline from nonstimulated vessels was not altered in the presence of nicotine. The effect of either compound could be counteracted by hexamethonium (but not by atropine); hexamethonium alone enhanced the transmitter release during the sympathetic nerve stimulation. Acetylcholine, released during stimulation of the perivascular cholinergic nerves of sympathetically denervated vessels would thus tend to inhibit the release of noradrenaline from the adjacent adrenergic nerves via a nicotinic type of cholinergic receptor (29). That a ganglionic mechanism might have been involved can be ruled out on an anatomical basis. Ganglion cells have never been observed in that part of the pial vasculature used in the experiments (6), and, accordingly, Borodulya and Pletchkova (31) only observed cholinergic ganglion formations in the intracranial portion of the internal carotid artery. Moreover, since nicotine alone did not affect the spontaneous efflux of tritium, and atropine did not counteract the inhibitory effect of nicotine on the electrically induced release of noradrenaline, it can be ruled out that the nicotinic receptors are located on the cholinergic axons running close along the adrenergic ones. Since the adrenergic sympathetic nerves appear to be under a vasoconstrictor tone (5), it follows that the cholinergic system, besides its direct (postjunctional) vasodilatory action mediated via the muscarinic receptors in the vascular smooth muscle, can promote pial vasodilation also indirectly, through a (prejunctional) inhibition of the noradrenaline release via the nicotinic receptors present on the perivascular sympathetic nerves. The interaction between the adrenergic and cholinergic systems has been confirmed in measurements of blood flow in the caudate nucleus of nonanesthetized rabbits utilizing the above-mentioned thermoclearance technique (32). A direct, dose-dependent increase in flow was achieved with carbamylcholine (infused at a rate of 2–4 μg/kg/min). Furthermore, this agent also produced a 50% inhibition of the flow reduction evoked by stimulation of the superior cervical ganglion. Such a mechanism should be distinguished from that which involves the well-known cholinergic (muscarinic) receptors on adrenergic nerve fibers in tissues lacking a direct innervation by cholinergic nerves, as recently discussed by Fozard and Muscholl (33); the physiological role of the latter arrangement seems less evident.

As mentioned above, histamine in high doses produces a cerebral vasoconstriction which does not involve specific histamine receptors (21). When this response is blocked by mepyramine, histamine is able to dilate isolated brain vessels (Fig. 4). This dilatory response, however, is inhibited in a competitive way by burimamide, showing that it is mediated by specific histamine receptors of the H_2 type. A similar response, though with a lower maximum effect, was obtained in extracranial arteries (Fig. 4), and the values for pA_2 (and K_B) obtained in experiments involving competitive reversible inhibition by burimamide were of the same order of magnitude as those reported for other tissues. The interesting action of histamine on the cerebral circulation thus appears to be the vasodilatation, which can be evoked at low doses and is blocked in a competitive manner by antihistaminic drugs.

Most investigations on the vascular action of 5-HT have focused on its vasoconstrictor effects, probably because of its suggested involvement in the development of cerebral vasospasm following subarachnoid hemorrhage, and because of the fact that it is the most potent vasoconstrictor known for brain vessels (22, 23). In the course of our studies on the characterization of receptors mediating the vasoconstrictor effects of 5-HT (24), it was found that this amine could also dilate both intracranial and extracranial arteries, provided they had been given an active tonic contraction beforehand by prostaglandin $F_{2\alpha}$, and the 5-HT induced contractile effects were blocked by exposure to phenoxybenzamine. Under these conditions, both 5-HT and tryptamine dilated the intracranial and extracranial vessels in a dose-dependent manner. The maximum effect of 5-HT was approximately 200 dyne, whereas the action of tryptamine on the intracranial vessels was much less pronounced. Judging from the ED_{50} values, 5-HT was more potent than tryptamine in its dilating effect on both types of vessels. Neither methysergide nor LSD was able to produce a parallel shift of the dose-response curves with 5-HT, but instead reduced the maximum effect successively without markedly affecting the ED_{50} value. The dilatory response of 5-HT could, on the other hand, be blocked in a competitive manner by increasing concentrations of two different β-receptor antagonists, propranolol and INPEA. The K_B values, and the corresponding value for

pA_2, were in the extracranial arteries similar to the corresponding values obtained with isoproterenol as agonist. In the intracranial circulation the pA_2 values for the dilatory action of 5-HT against the two β-antagonists were found to be intermediary between those obtained for the dilatation by isoproterenol in middle cerebral arteries (16) and those for isoproterenol-induced effects in peripheral tissues (28). This supports previous evidence suggesting that intracranial vascular β-receptors are different from those in the extracranial vascular bed.

CONCLUDING REMARKS

The well-developed adrenergic and cholinergic innervation of the cerebrovascular system is described in relation to the characteristics of several amine receptors mediating contractile and dilatory functions in the vessels, and comparison is made with the corresponding receptors in the extracranial circulation. Because of the limited space, this discussion is mainly based on results obtained in our own laboratory. A more comprehensive review of amine mechanisms in the cerebrovascular bed has recently appeared (34), and full reference to work from other laboratories is given in this and in the original articles mentioned in the present paper.

A rather detailed understanding of the various receptor mechanisms mediating the effects of perivascular nerves and several vasoactive amines on cerebral blood flow is now beginning to develop. The complex situation is summarized in Fig. 7. It is a general impression that there are a number of major differences in the reactivity of cerebral vessels as compared to vasomotor functions in the peripheral circulation. These are reflected in quantitative as well as qualitative differences in the characteristics of the pharmacological receptors. Since this type of knowledge forms the basis for a more physiological approach to the investigations of neurogenic and aminergic control mechanisms in the cerebrovascular bed, it is important to realize that it will not be possible to design proper experiments by simple extrapolation of experience

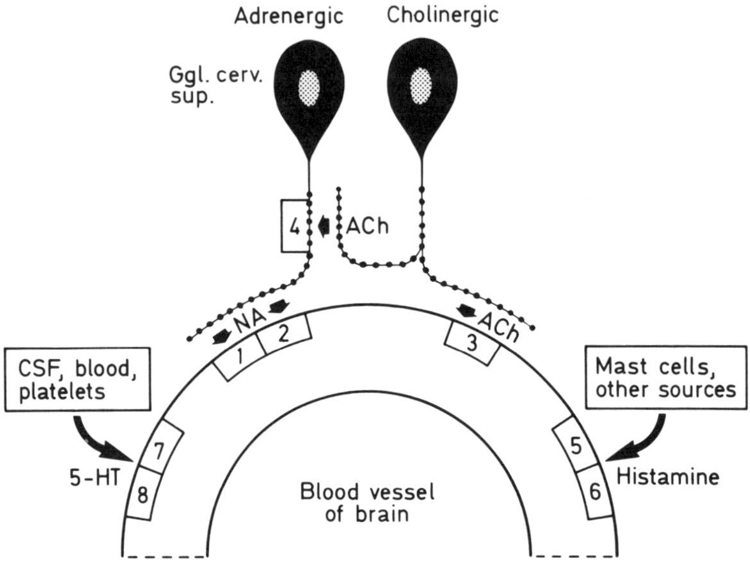

Receptor No.	Receptor type	Response	Inhibitors tested	Mode of inhibition	pA_2
1	alpha	+	piperoxan phentolamine	competitive (reversible)	7.06
			phenoxybenzamine dibenamine	competitive (irreversible)	
2	$beta_1$	—	propranolol INPEA practolol	competitive	9.17
3	muscarinic	— and +	atropine	competitive	10.43 and 10.07
4	nicotinic	—	hexamethonium	competitive	
5	histamine (non-spec.)	+	mepyramine chlorpheniramine	non-competitive	
6	histamine H_2	—	burimamide	competitive	5.51
7	serotonin	+	methysergide LSD	non-competitive (reversible)	
8	beta (serotonin)	—	methysergide LSD	non-competitive	
			propranolol INPEA	competitive	8.29 8.47

+, contraction; —, dilation (inhibition in case of nicotinic receptors)

Fig. 7. Schematic representation of the postganglionic autonomic innervation and other sources of amines acting on brain vessels, together with the corresponding receptors and some of their pharmacological characteristics, including the values for pA_2, which express competitive antagonist affinity (pA_2 is the same for a given antagonist acting on a particular receptor irrespective of the agonist used).

obtained in earlier work on receptor identification and characterization in the peripheral vascular bed. Moreover, it is now evident that nerve systems other than the aminergic ones, i.e. peptide nerves, may mediate vascular actions in the brain, and that the neurogenic and so-called metabolic mechanisms may interact in a control function of the cerebral blood flow.

REFERENCES

1. Samarasinghe DD: The innervation of the cerebral arteries in the rat: an electron microscope study. J Anat 99:815–828, 1965.
2. Pease DC, Molinari S: Electron microscopy of muscular arteries; Pial vessels of the cat and monkey. J Ultrastruct Res 3:447–468, 1960.
3. Falck B: Observations on the possibilities of the cellular localization of monoamines by a fluorescence method. Acta Physol Scand 56(Suppl. 197):1–25, 1962.
4. Owman Ch, Edvinsson L, Falck B, Nielsen KC: Amine mechanisms in brain vessels, with particular regard to autonomic innervation and blood-brain barrier. In Cervos-Navarro J (ed): "Pathology of Cerebral Microcirculation." Berlin/New York: Walter de Gruyter, 1974, pp 184–200.
5. Sercombe R, Aubineau P, Edvinsson L, Mamo H, Owman Ch, Pinard E, Seylaz J: Neurogenic influence on local cerebral blood flow. Effect of catecholamines or sympathetic nerve stimulation as correlated with the sympathetic innervation. Neurology 25:954–963, 1975.
6. Edvinsson L, Nielsen KC, Owman Ch, Sporrong B: Cholinergic mechanisms in pial vessels. Histochemisty, electron microscopy and pharamacology. Z Zellforsch 134:311–325, 1972.
7. Larsson L-I, Edvinsson L, Fahrenkrug J, Håkanson R, Owman Ch, Schaffalitzky De Muckadell O, Sundler F: Immunohistochemical localization of a vasodilatory polypeptide (VIP) in cerebrovascular nerves. Brain Res 113:400–404, 1976.
8. Lee TJ-F, Su C, Bevan JA: Nonsympathetic dilator innervation of cat cerebral arteries. Experientia 31:1424–1425, 1975.
9. Lindvall M, Cervos-Navarro J, Edvinsson L, Owman Ch, Stenevi U: Non-sympathetic perivascular nerves in the brain: Origin and mode of innervation studied by fluorescence and electron microscopy combined with stereotaxic lesions and sympathectomy. In Harper AM, Jennett WB, Miller JD, Rowan JO (eds): "Blood Flow and Metabolism in the Brain." Edinburgh: Churchill Livingstone, 1975, pp 1.7–1.9.
10. Pool JD: Cerebral vasospasm. N Engl J Med 259:1259–1264, 1958.

11. Rennels ML, Nelson E: Capillary innervation in the mammalian central nervous system: An electron microscopic demonstration. Am J Anat 144:233–241, 1975.
12. Owman Ch, Edvinsson L, Hardebo JE, Gröschel-Stewart U, Unsicker K, Walles B: Immunohistochemical demonstration of actin and myosin in brain capillaries. Acta Neurol Scand (Suppl 64)56:384–385, 1977.
13. Edvinsson L, Hardebo JE, Owman Ch: Role of perivascular sympathetic nerves in autoregulation of cerebral blood flow and in blood-brain barrier functions. Acta Neurol Scand (Suppl 64)56:50–51, 1977.
14. Edvinsson L, Aubineau P, Owman Ch, Sercombe R, Seylaz J: Sympathetic innervation of cerebral arteries: Prejunctional supersensitivity to norepinephrine after sympathectomy or cocaine treatment. Stroke 6:525–530, 1975.
15. Bevan JA, Bevan RD: Localized neurogenic vasoconstriction of the basilar artery. Stroke 4:760–763, 1973.
16. Edvinsson L, Owman Ch: Pharmacological characterization of adrenergic alpha and beta receptors mediating vasomotor responses of cerebral arteries in vitro. Cir Res 35:835–849, 1974.
17. Edvinsson L, Sercombe R: Influence of pH and pCO_2 on alpha-receptor mediated contraction in brain vessels. Acta Physiol Scand 97:325–331, 1976.
18. Svendgaard N-A, Edvinsson L, Owman Ch: Increased pial artery sensitivity to norepinephrine and 5-hydroxytryptamine following experimental subarachnoid hemorrhage. Surg Neurol (In press).
19. Edvinsson L, Owman Ch, Sahlin C, Svendgaard N-A: Changes in uptake and accumulation of norepinephrine in sympathetic nerves of pial vessels following experimental subarachnoid hemorrhage. J Neurosurg (In press).
20. Edvinsson L, Cervos-Navarro J, Larsson L-I, Owman Ch, Rönnberg A-L: Regional distribution of mast cells containing histamine, dopamine or 5-hydroxytryptamine in the mammalian brain. Neurology 27:878–883, 1977.
21. Edvinsson L, Owman Ch: A pharmacological comparison of histamine receptors in isolated extracranial and intracranial arteries in vitro. Neurology 25:271–276, 1975.
22. Nielsen KC, Owman Ch: Contractile response and amine receptor mechanisms in isolated middle cerebral artery of the cat. Brain Res 27:33–42, 1971.
23. Allen GS, Henderson LM, Chou SN, French LA: Cerebral arterial spasm. Part 2: In vitro contractile activity of serotonin in human serum and CSF on the canine basilar artery, and its blockage by methysergide and phenoxybenzamine. J Neurosurg 40:442–450, 1974.

24. Edvinsson L, Hardebo JE, Owman Ch: Pharmacological analysis of 5-hydroxytryptamine receptors in isolated intracranial and extracranial vessels of cat and man. Circ Res (In press).
25. Gyermek L: Drug which antagonizes 5-hydroxytryptamine and related indoleaylamines. In Eichler O, Farah A (eds): "Handbook of Experimental Pharmacology." New York: Springer-Verlag, 1966, Vol 29, pp 471–528.
26. Zervas NT, Kuwayama A, Rosoff CB, Salzman EW: Cerebral arterial spasm. Modification in inhibition of platelet function. Arch Neurol 28:400–404, 1973.
27. Sercombe R, Aubineau P, Edvinsson L, Mamo H, Owman Ch, Seylaz J: Pharmacological evidence in vitro and in vivo for functional $beta_1$ receptors in the cerebral circulation. Pflügers Arch 368:241–244, 1977.
28. Furchgott RF: The classification of adrenoceptors (adrenergic receptors). An evaluation from the standpoint of receptor theory. In Blaschko H, Muscholl E (eds): "Handbook of Experimental Pharmacology." Berlin-Heidelberg-New York: Springer-Verlag, 1972, pp 283–335.
29. Edvinsson L, Falck B, Owman Ch: Possibilities for a cholinergic action on smooth musculature and on sympathetic axons in brain vessels mediated by muscarinic and nicotinic receptors. J Pharmacol Exp Ther 200:117–126, 1977.
30. Burgen ASV, Emmelin NG: Physiology of the salivary glands. In Barcroft H, Davson H, Paton WDM (eds): "Monographs of the Physiological Society." London: Edward Arnold, 1961, pp 1–279.
31. Borodulya AV, Pletchkova EK: Distribution of cholinergic and adrenergic nerves in the internal carotid artery. Acta Anat 86: 410–425, 1973.
32. Aubineau P, Sercombe R: Evidence for a double cholinergic mechanism capable of reducing the tone of cerebral arteries. Acta Neurol Scand (Suppl 64)56:296–297, 1977.
33. Fozard JR, Muscholl E: Do adrenergic fibres have muscarinic inhibitory receptors? – A reply. J Pharm Pharmacol 26:662–664, 1974.
34. Edvinsson L, Mackenzie E: Amine mechanisms in the cerebral circulation. Pharmacol Rev 28:275–353, 1976.

6. Concluding Remarks

Eugene Roberts and Peter Amacher

The purpose of this meeting was to accelerate the work that would test the validity of the use of propranolol in the treatment of individuals suffering from schizophrenia or other types of psychoses. This purpose was well served in that at least two of the participants, Pitts and Van Kammen, developed new research protocols at their respective institutions where work is now in progress in suitably controlled studies. The latter individuals benefited from in-depth discussions with the two groups that presented their results at the meeting, both with regard to precautions and research design. In addition, notice given in the medical and scientific circles concerned with the treatment of mental disorders has stimulated a number of individuals to query those with experience in the use of propranolol in psychiatry with regard to the available data on the research conducted to date. Some of the original observations were published in rather obscure journals, and all of the work has not been available in one place for perusal by those interested. We hope that the publication of this book will fill an information gap.

The proceedings were opened impressively by the showing of a videotape made in England of several patients before treatment and during treatment with the drug. This gave those present a common appreciation for the problems involved and the kinds of improvements that were possible in patients who had not been helped by other treatment modalities. The

Propranolol and Schizophrenia, pages 149–150

caution exercised by Yorkston in presenting the material and his concern for the welfare and privacy of the individuals being studied was truly impressive and typical of the whole approach of the British group.

A second videotape showed the results of a double-blind withdrawal study, a consequence of an administrative decision. Distressing reversals of the results shown on the first tape were seen.

The meeting was not a "selling" session. Both groups of researchers constantly were cautioning the others in attendance not to become overly enthusiastic at this point in the work. Yorkston reminded us several times that there had been many false dawns in schizophrenia research, and that this field had been the graveyard of the reputations of many psychiatrists. Nevertheless, the optimism of both groups came through, and it was evident from the presentations that they believed that they had genuinely seen exciting therapeutic results. Since the time of the meeting, the results of the open studies have been confirmed by Yorkston and colleagues (1) in controlled double-blind studies with 14 patients, and the edge has been removed from the criticism that the validity of the findings was in question until such studies were performed.

We feel that, even if it is not a new dawn, the findings presented in this volume might provide a lifting of the fog that obscures our understanding of these disorders.

REFERENCES

1. Yorkston NJ, Gruzelier JH, Zaki SA, Hollander D, Pitcher DR, Sergeant HGS: Propranolol as an adjunct to the treatment of schizophrenia. Lancet (In Press). Also in this volume pp 69–82.

Index